천상병 — 귀천

Back to Heaven

Selected Poems of **Ch'ŏn Sang Pyŏng**
Translated by Brother Anthony of Taizé / Kim Young-Moo

도서출판 답게

한국문학영역총서

Back to Heaven

Translated by Brother Anthony and Kim Young-Moo

이 책은 Cornell East Asia Series No. 77로 1995년에 미국 코넬대학에서 간행된 바 있는 *Back to Heaven*의 한국어 대역판으로, 도서출판 답게와 Cornell East Asia Series와의 공동출판 형식으로 나온 것임을 밝힙니다.

This bilingual edition is a joint publication of DapGae Publishing Company and the Cornell University East Asia Program. An English language only version including more poems was originally published in 1995 under the same title as number 77 in the Cornell East Asia Series(ISSN 1050-2955), Cornell University East Asia Program, 140 Uris Hall, Ithaca, NY 14853-7601, ISBN 0-885445-69-5 cloth, ISBN 0-885445-77-6 paper.

Original Poems ⓒ Ch'ŏn Sang Pyŏng
Translation ⓒ 1996, Brother Anthony and Kim Young-Moo

Published by DapGae Books
#2F 469-10, Gunja-Dong, Gwangjin-Gu, Seoul, 143-838, Korea
Tel/ (02)462-0464, 463-0464 Fax /(02)498-0463

Cornell East Asia Program
Cornell University
Ithaca, New York 14853

Printed and bound in the Republic of Korea
No. 77, Cornell East Asia Series ISSN 1050-2955
Cornell East Asia Program ISBN 0-885445-69-5 cloth, ISBN 0-885445-77-6 paper.

Dap Gae
English Translations of Korean Literature Series
Editor : Kim Young-Moo

머리말

　천상병 시인은 1993년 4월 28일 세상을 떠났는데, 그것은 오래 전에 예행 연습이 끝난 죽음이었다. 그가 처음 세상을 떠난 것은 1967년 중앙정보부 요원들이 서울 중심부에 있는 그들의 본부인 그 무시무시한 지하실로 그를 끌고 갔을 때였다. 그는 거기서 물 고문과, 성기에 전기 충격을 가하는 전기 고문을 받았다. 간첩 혐의로 기소된 대학 시절 친구의 수첩에서 그의 이름이 발견되었기 때문이었다. 천상병은 여섯 달을 갇혀 있다가 풀려났다. 자백을 강요받았으나 친구가 여럿 있다는 사실 말고는 자백할 것이 없었다. 이때의 전기 고문으로 그는 자식을 가질 수 없는 몸이 되었다.
　1930년 일본 땅에서 태어난 그는 해방되던 해, 가족을 따라 귀국하여 마산에서 학업을 계속했다. 그가 아직 학생이던 1949년 월간 잡지 《문예》에 그의 첫 작품 「강물」이 발표되었다. 서울대학교에서 공부를 하던 1952년경에는 이미 추천이 완료되어 그는 기성 시인 대접을 받았다. 대학을 졸업하고 그는 잠시 부산에서 일을 했는데, 시를 쓰는 한편으로 문학평론을 여러 잡지에 발표하기 시작하면서 평론 활동도 그의 작가로서의 생활에 중요한 일부분을 이룬다.
　고문을 받은 사건이 있은 후 얼마 되지 않아서, 천상병은 또 한 번 '죽음'을 맞게 된다. 고문의 깊은 후유증에 시달리며 술타령으로 나날을 떠돌던 그가 마침내 1971년 실종된 것이다. 친구와 친척들은 여러 달 동안 백방으로 그를 찾아보았지만 허사였다. 행려병자로 사망하여 아무도 모르는 어디엔가 파묻힌 것으로 결론을 내린 그들은, 비통한 심정으로 그의 작품들을 모아 유고 시집을 발간했다.

여러 차례의 죽음으로 점철된 것이 천상병의 생애라면, 그의 삶은 또한 여러 겹의 부활의 이야기이기도 하다. 그가 살아 있다는, 서울의 시립 정신병원에 입원해 있다는 느닷없는 소식이 왔다. 그는 거리에서 쓰러져 그 병원으로 이송되었는데, 그때 그는 자신의 이름과 자신이 시인이라는 사실 말고는 아무 것도 기억하지 못했다. 이 두 번째 기억이 그의 생명의 끈이었는지도 모를 일이다.

심한 자폐증상을 보이는 가운데서도, 대학 때 친구의 여동생인 목순옥의 방문을 받은 뒤로는 그의 병세가 호전되기 시작했다. 의사는 그녀에게 자주 찾아오는 것이 도움이 되며 모든 것이 잘 되면 한두 달 뒤에 퇴원할 수 있을 거라고 말해주었다. 그래서 목순옥은 오빠의 친구를 매일 방문하게 되었고, 마침내 그는 사회로 복귀할 수 있는 상태가 되었다. 다만 그에게는 스스로를 부양할 능력이 없다는 것이 문제였다. 그는 철없는 어린애 같았고 어린애처럼 약했다. 천상병과 목순옥은 1972년 결혼을 하게 되고, 이들의 결혼생활은 때로는 심한 고난과 어려움을 겪으며 20년 간 계속된다.

친구들을 좋아하고 그냥 아무나 믿으며 술과 담배를 즐기는 그의 성품으로는 신혼부부의 의식주를 해결하는 데 아무런 도움도 되지 못했다. 친구들의 도움으로 목순옥은 서울 인사동 골목에 작은 찻집을 열었고, 예술인, 작가, 언론인, 지식인들이 단골 손님이 되었다. 천상병 시인의 초기 작품 중 하나의 제목을 따서 이 찻집의 옥호를 '귀천歸天'이라 불렀다. 이들 부부는 서울 북쪽 교외로 나가 의정부에 있는 낡은 가옥의 작은 방에서 살림을 시작했다.

술에 곯은 시인의 간장이 성할 리가 없었다. 1988년 목순옥은 의사로부터 남편의 시련이 막바지에 이르렀으며 결코 회복할 가망이 없으니 불가피한 임종에 대비하라는 얘기를 들었다. 춘천에서 개업하고 있는 의사인 친구가 그들을 돕기로 했다. 천상병은 곧 입원했고 목순옥은 그 뒤 여러 달 동안 버스를 타고 춘천까지 달려가 매일 저녁을 그와 함께 보냈다. 그녀는 매일 춘천에서 돌아오는 길에 버스 안에서 이런 기도를 드렸다고 적고 있다. "하느님! 아직은 안 됩니다. 그에게 5년만 더 주십시오. 제발 빕니다. 5년만 더요."

놀랍게도 그는 원기를 되찾았고, 그 뒤 퇴원하여 그럭저럭 정상적인 생활을 할 수 있게 되었다. 5년 동안이었다. 이 유예의 기간 중에 그의 새로운 시집들과 에세이집들이 출간되었고, 1993년 4월 28일 그는 마지막 귀천 길에 올랐다. 이제 인사동 찻집 문을 열어도, 늘 그가 앉던 자리에서 들려오던 시인의 꺼칠한 목소리를 들을 수 없게 되었다. 열다섯 명만 들어와도 꽉 차는 그곳이 만원일 때에도 그는 말했다. "어서 와요, 여기 자리 있어요, 여기요!"

천상병은 되살아나서 자신의 유고 시집의 출판을 목격하는 진귀한 특권을 누렸으며, 여기서 그치지 않고 그의 첫 유고 시집 이후에 몇 권의 시집을 더 출판할 수 있었다. 그의 두 번째 유고 시집, 이번에는 진짜인 유고 시집이 간행된 것은 1993년이었다.

천상병은 어떤 종류의 시를 썼는가? 자신의 주위 세상에 대해 사사롭게 보고 느낀 것을 적은 서정시가 주류를 이룬다. 그리고 그가 깊은 친화력을 느꼈던 주위 환경은 자연 세계이다. 인간의 세상은 좀 더 복잡한 세계여서, 그가 마음놓을 수 있었던 친구들과 아내를 찬양하는 시편들이 있을 뿐, 자신과는 아주 낯선 세계에 사는 많은 사람들, 가령, 재물을 얻으려고 바쁜 사람들에 대한 분명한 언급은 별로 없다.

이 시인의 작품세계의 원천이 되고 있는 현실인식은 지극히 인간적이고 섬세하고 때로는 거의 신비적이다. 나이가 들어가면서 그의 시에서는 하느님이 점점 더 분명한 모습을 드러내며, 예수께서 가난한 자를 반기시고 부유한 자를 내치시는 복음서의 메아리가 들려온다. 천상병 시인의 마음은 마지막까지 어린이의 마음이었고 삶에 대한 그의 반응도 어린애 같았으며, 그의 믿음 또한 어린이다운 가벼움으로 드러난다.

   한국의 현대시가 대개 그렇듯이, 그의 시행의 움직임은 매우 자유롭고, 문법에 얽매이지 않으며, 소리 내서 읽을 때 더욱 효과가 난다. 한국 문학은 때때로 경전을 중시하는 문인 전통에 뿌리를 내리는 경우가 있는데, 그의 어조는 이보다는 훨씬 구어체의 목소리에 가깝다고 할 수 있다. 대체로 아주 간단한 낱말들이 동원되고 있어서, 시의 핵심을 이루는 체험들은 같은 생각을 가진 독자들이 함께 느낌을 공유하는 식으로 전달되는 경우가 흔하다. 그것은 부모님의 묘지를 찾아가려는데 기차표 살 돈이 없어 서울을 뜨지 못하면서 하늘에 갈 차비를 벌어야 한다면 어떻게 해야 하나 하고 궁리하는 경우에 드러나는 것과 같은 억지 웃음일 때도 있고, 강렬한 행복감일 때도, 비오는 날의 우수일 때도 있다.

   어떤 시들은 너무 단순, 소박해서 겉으로 드러난 그 천진성에 기가 막혀 현학적인 비평가들은 모욕감을 느낄 수도 있을 것이다. 시는 고급 예술이고 매우 진지한 것인데, "이런 시는 유치원에서도 쓸 수 있는 것 아닌가" 하고 불평을 할 수도 있을 것이다. 물론 천상병이야말로 그의 시대의 시인 가운데 거의 유일하게 완전히 정직한 시인이라고 말하는 학생들이나 많은 독자들과 생각을 같이 하는 비평가들도 있다. 그들의 생각이 틀린 것은 아니다. 천상병의 모든 작품은 그 깊은 진정성으로 우리의 심금을 울려준다. 그가 쓴 대부분의 것들은 다른 사람이라면 결코 쓸 수 없는 종류의 것들이다.

   그의 일생은 가난과 고통으로 물든 삶이었다. 그런데도 낱낱의 시들이 하나같이 때로는 분명하게 "나는 세상에서 가장 행복한 사나이"라고 선언한다. 그의 시는 자신이 받은 복을 귀하게 여기며, 그것이 진정 무엇인지를 깨닫고, 삶의 참맛을 음미하면서, 어두운 그림자 같은 것은 쫓을 염도 내지 않는 사람에게서 나오는 노래들이다. 물론 그림자들도 있다. 죽음이야말로 가장 어두운 그림자가 아닌가. 죽음과 인간의 유한성이라는 현실은 천상병이 처음 발표한 시 「강물」에서 바다를 향해 흐르는 강물의 흐름으로 상징되어 나타난다. 다만 목숨이 있는 한 우리는 죽은 것이 아니며, 천상병은 살아있는 사람으로 쓸 뿐이다. 너무 생생히 살아 있어서 새들의 울음소리 하나 하나, 떨어지는 나뭇잎 하나 하나에도 그의 마음은 열리는 것이다.

가난한 사람은 행복하다는 예수님 말씀의 참뜻을 그의 시들은 완벽하게 보여준다. 부자들은 자신들이 못 가진 것들에 대해 불평을 하지만, 가난한 사람들은 그들이 가진 얼마 안 되는 작은 것에서 무한한 기쁨을 느낀다. 들꽃 한 다발이면 더 바랄 것이 없는 것이다. 부유한 사람들은 여기 있는 시 한편 한편을 압도적인 것으로 만들고 있는 것들, 즉 세상의 아름다움, 이 아름다운 세상에 살아있는 아름다움에 눈멀어 있다. 여기 있는 시들이 아름다운 까닭은 대체로 그것들이 굳이 아름다운 것이 되려고 애쓰지 않기 때문이다. 시인이 느낀 아름다움이, 잘 짜여진 언어의 구조 속에서 그냥 빛나도록 놔두고 있는 것이 그의 작품들이다.

시인은 인간 사회가 얼마나 추악한 세상인지 너무나 잘 알고 있으며, 그의 시들은 그런 세상에 대한 예술의 승리를 증언하고 있다. 적어도 15세기에 프랑소아 비용이 파리의 거리를 떠돌았던 이래로 방랑 시인이란 인기 있는 문사인데, 20세기 서울 사람들이 가졌던 방랑 시인은 비용보다 더한 슬픔과 고통을 자신의 놀이로 가까이했음에도, 그보다는 더 큰 순수성을 지니고 있었다. 그는 정녕 행복한 사람이었다. 그를 그렇게 돌보아준 훌륭한 아내가 있었으니 더더욱 행복한 사람이었다.

자신이 죽은 지 몇 달 뒤 그들이 함께 한 삶의 눈부신 회고록이 아내에 의해 출판될 것에 생각이 미쳤다면, 천상병은 기뻐했을 것이다. 흐뭇해하거나 조금은 놀랐을 것이다. 그 뒤 어떤 희곡 작가가 그들의 삶의 주요 사건들을 엮은 연극 대본을 썼고, 그의 시

몇 편이 코러스로 읽혀진 이 연극의 공연은 여러 주일 동안 객석을 가득 가득 채웠다. 연극 '귀천'에 대한 사람들의 열렬한 반응은, 그의 시집의 폭발적인 판매 부수와 더불어, 천상병이 의정부의 작은 언덕 위 무덤 속에 묻혔지만, 결코 '죽은 시인'이 아님을 드러내는 가장 분명한 표지가 아니고 무엇이겠는가. 여러 해 전에 쓴 그의 가장 아름다운 시 「귀천」에서 그가 약속했던 대로 천상병은 뭇 사람들의 가슴속에 있는 하늘로 돌아갔다.

> 나 하늘로 돌아가리라
> 아름다운 이 세상 소풍 끝내는 날,
> 가서, 아름다웠더라고 말하리라……

여기에 그 일생 작업의 비밀이 있다. 세상은 아름답다는 것, 인생은 아름답다는 것, 우리는 매일 기뻐해야 한다는 것을, 그는 들을 귀가 있는 이들에게 가르치고 있는 것이다.

Introduction

When Ch'ŏn Sang Pyŏng left this world on April 28, 1993, it was a long-rehearsed departure. He had already left the world a first time in 1967, when the agents of the National Security Agency whisked him away to the dreaded cellars of their building in central Seoul. There he was subjected to torture by water, and also by electric-shock applied to his genitals. His name had been found in the address-book of a friend from university days, a friend who was now accused of being a communist spy. After six months in detention, he was finally freed, having nothing to confess except the fact that he had friends. As a result of the electrical torture, the poet would never be able to have children.

Born in early 1930 in Japan, he returned to Korea with his family in 1945 and resumed his interrupted schooling at Masan. The first of his poems to be published was the poem "River waters" that appeared in the monthly review *Munye* in 1949, when the poet was still at school. By 1952 he was established as a poet, with recognition from already reputed writers. By this time he was studying at Seoul National University. After finishing his studies there, he worked for a while in Pusan. In addition to writing poems, he had also already begun to compose literary essays that were published in various periodicals. They constitute the other important aspect of his life's work as a writer.

Not very long after being tortured, Ch'ŏn Sang Pyŏng "died" a second time. Deeply traumatized by the violence he had undergone, he began to roam about, drinking wildly until at last, in 1971, he disappeared. Months passed, his friends and relatives searched for him everywhere to no avail. They could only conclude that he had died and been buried somewhere anonymously, unknown. In sorrow, they collected the poems they could find, and published a posthumous memorial volume.

Ch'ŏn Sang Pyŏng's career may have been marked by a series of deaths, it is also a story of multiple resurrections. Suddenly news came that he was alive after all, interned in the Seoul municipal asylum where he had been taken after he had collapsed in the street. The only things he could recall at that time were his name, and the fact that he was a poet. Perhaps the second memory was the thread that kept him alive.

Deeply withdrawn though he was, Ch'ŏn Sang Pyŏng showed a clear improvement after being visited by Mok Sun Ok, the younger sister of one of his university friends. The doctor told her that she could help him by her visits and that if all went well he might be ready to return to life in the outside world after a couple of months. So Mok Sun Ok came to visit her brother's friend every day, until he was as ready as he ever would be to come back to life in society. Only it was clear that he would hardly be able to fend for himself on his own. He had the heart of a child, and a child's fragility. Ch'ŏn Sang Pyŏng and Mok Sun Ok were married in 1972, a marriage that endured through twenty years of sometimes terrible hardship and struggle.

The poet's love of company, his simple trust, and his enjoyment of a drink and a smoke, did not answer the question of how the newly-weds were to feed and house themselves. Friends helped Mok Sun Ok open a café in a small room in the Insadong neighborhood of Seoul, much frequented by artists, writers, journalists and intellectuals. The name given to the café was *Kwi–*

ch'ŏn "Back to heaven," the title of one of Ch'ŏn's early lyrics. The couple lived in tiny rooms in an old house on the outskirts of Uijŏngbu, to the north of Seoul.

By 1988, years of drinking had eroded the poet's liver until at last a doctor told Mok Sun Ok that her husband had reached the end of the trail, that he would never recover and she must prepare for the inevitable end. Another doctor, a friend of theirs, with a small clinic in the town of Ch'unch'ŏn, twenty or thirty miles outside of Seoul, decided to try to help. Ch'ŏn Sang Pyŏng was admitted there and for the following months Mok Sun Ok took the bus every evening to be with him. She has written how, returning to Seoul from her daily visits, she used to pray silently in the bus: "God! Not yet. Give him another five years, please. Five more years."

Amazingly, strength returned and the poet was able to leave the clinic to resume a measure of normal living. For another five years. In the space of this reprieve he saw the publication of new volumes of poetry and of essays. Until at last he made his final journey Back to Heaven on April 28, 1993. People opening the door of the Insadong café no longer hear the poet's raucous voice call from his customary seat in a corner: "Come on in, there's room, there's room!" Even when, with fifteen customers, the room was completely full.

Ch'ŏn Sang Pyŏng enjoyed the rare privilege of surviving to see his poems published posthumously; more than that, his first, "posthumous" volume of poems was followed by several other volumes published in his lifetime. In 1993 a second, this time truly posthumous, volume of poems appeared.

* * *

What kind of poetry did Ch'ŏn Sang Pyŏng write? Essentially lyric verse echoing his private perceptions of the world around him. Often it is the world of nature, with which he feels a deep harmony. The world of human society is more complex. There are poems celebrating the people he feels at ease with, his friends, his wife. There are less obvious references to the many people who live in ways quite foreign to him: people busy in pursuit of wealth, for example.

The perception of reality out of which the poet's works spring is deeply human, sensitive and sometimes almost mystical. With the passage of time "God" figures more and more explicitly in his poems, with echoes of the passages in the Gospels where Jesus welcomes the poor and excludes the rich. Ch'ŏn Sang Pyŏng's heart was to the end the heart of a child and his response to life is childlike, his faith too is expressed with a childlike lightness.

As is usual in modern Korean poetry, the movement of the lines is very free, grammar is loose, the poems benefit greatly from being read aloud. They are much closer to the speaking voice than is sometimes the case with Korean literature, rooted as it is in a scholarly tradition of the written text. Using mostly a very simple vocabulary, the experience at the core of each poem is usually conveyed to the sympathetic reader as a shared emotion. It may be a wry smile, as when the poet is stranded in Seoul without the train fare to go to visit his parents' tombs and he wonders what he will do if he has to find the fare to go to heaven. Or it may be an intense happiness. Or the gloom of a rainy day.

Some poems are so simple, that over-sophisticated critics feel insulted by the apparent childishness. Poetry is supposed to be high art, deeply serious, and they complain: "But this could have been written in a nursery school." Only it wasn't. There are others who agree with the students' and general readers' opinion that Ch'ŏn Sang Pyŏng was almost the only utterly honest writer of his generation. They are not wrong. Everything he wrote strikes one as deeply authentic. Most of what he wrote could not have been written by anyone else.

His biography suggests a life steeped in poverty and pain. Yet poem after poem proclaims, sometimes explicitly: "I'm the happiest man in the world." These are songs of a man who counts his blessings and knows exactly what they are, who relishes life and refuses any thought of running after shadows. Shadows there were, of course, death being the darkest one. Death and human mortality are the realities symbolized in the flow of the river towards the sea in the poet's first published poem, "River waters." Only we're not dead so long as we're alive, and Ch'ŏn writes as a man alive, so alive that his heart is wide open to the song of every bird, the fall of every leaf.

The poems illustrate perfectly what Christ meant when he said that the poor were blessed. The rich complain about all they don't have; the poor rejoice intensely in the few simple things they have; a bunch of wild flowers is enough. The rich are blind to what makes poem after poem so compelling: the beauty of the world, the beauty of being alive in this beautiful world. These poems are mostly very beautiful because they do not try to be. They let the beauty that the poet has perceived shine through their fabric of finely spun words.

The poet knew well enough how very ugly the world of human

society could be, his poems are a witness to the victory of art over that. The vagabond poet has been a popular literary figure at least since François Villon roamed and played in 15th century Paris. 20th century Seoul had a poet whose games were closer to sorrow and pain than Villon's perhaps, but whose reserves of innocence were greater too. A happy man, indeed, and the happier for having had such a wonderful wife to look after him.

Ch'ŏn Sang Pyŏng would have been delighted, if amused and a little surprised, at the thought that only a few months after his death his wife would have published a splendid book of memoirs about their life together. Then a writer composed a play portraying the main events of their life, with readings of some of the poems serving as the Chorus, that drew crowded houses for several weeks in a Seoul theater. The popular response to the play *Kwi-chon* is the clearest sign, together with the explosion of sales of his books, that Ch'ŏn Sang Pyŏng is no "dead poet," despite having a tomb on a hill in Uijŏngbu. He has gone Back to Heaven inside many hearts, and as he promised in that most beautiful poem, *Kwi-ch'ŏn*, "Back to Heaven", written many years ago:

> I'll go back to heaven again.
> At the end of my outing to this beautiful world
> I'll go back and say : It was beautiful...

There is the secret of his life's work. He teaches those ready to listen that the world is beautiful, that life is beautiful, and that we ought every day to be glad.

Brother Anthony

차례
Contents

새
Bird (1971)

피리 · 24	25 · Flute
나무 · 26	27 · Tree
갈매기 · 28	29 · Seagull
약속 · 30	31 · Rendez-vous
갈대 · 32	33 · Reed
다음 · 34	35 · Next
강물 · 36	37 · River waters
푸른 것만이 아니다 · 38	39 · Not just blue
덕수궁의 오후 · 40	41 · One afternoon in Tŏksu Palace
새 · 42	43 · Bird
새 2 · 44	45 · Bird 2
새 3 · 46	47 · Bird 3
주막에서 · 48	49 · In a tavern
새 · 50	51 · Bird
곡哭 신동엽 · 52	53 · Lament for Shin Dong-yŏp
주일 1 · 54	55 · Sabbath 1
주일 2 · 56	57 · Sabbath 2
회상 1 · 58	59 · Memories
편지 · 60	61 · Letter
진혼가 · 62	63 · Requiem

국화꽃 · 64	65 · One chrysanthemum
회상 2 · 66	67 · Memories 2
아가야 · 68	69 · Little child
음악 · 70	71 · Music
귀천 · 72	73 · Back to Heaven
들국화 · 74	75 · Daisies
한낮의 별빛 · 76	77 · Daytime starlight
"크레이지 배가본드" · 78	79 · "Crazy Vagabond"
미소 · 80	81 · Smile
나의 가난은 · 82	83 · My poverty
간의 반란 · 84	85 · Liver revolt
넋 · 86	87 · Soul
한 가지 소원 · 88	89 · One Wish
만추晩秋 · 90	91 · Late Autumn
소릉조小陵調 · 92	93 · A La Tu Fu
그날은 · 94	95 · That day
꽃의 위치에 대하여 · 96	97 · The place of flowers
광화문에서 · 98	99 · At Kwanghwa-mun

주막에서
In a tavern(1978)

눈 · 102	103 ·	*Eyes*
내 집 · 104	105 ·	*My house*
비 7 · 106	107 ·	*Rain 7*
비 8 · 108	109 ·	*Rain 8*
비 11 · 110	111 ·	*Rain 11*
비 · 112	113 ·	*Rain*
봄소식 · 118	119 ·	*News of spring*
8월의 종소리 · 120	121 ·	*August bell*
시냇물가 5 · 122	123 ·	*Streamside 5*
인생서가人生序歌 · 124	125 ·	*Prelude to life*
선경仙境 1 · 126	127 ·	*Fairyland 1*
동창同窓 · 128	129 ·	*Classmates*
길 · 130	131 ·	*Road*
약수터 · 132	133 ·	*Beside a spring*
기쁨 · 134	135 ·	*Joy*
희망 · 136	137 ·	*Hope*
길 · 138	139 ·	*Road*
흰구름 · 140	141 ·	*White cloud*
꽃은 훈장 · 142	143 ·	*A flower's a medal*
무덤 · 144	145 ·	*Tombs*

천상 시인
A Real Poet(1984)

날개 · 148	149 · Wings
먼산山 · 150	151 · Distant mountain
고향 · 152	153 · Home
구름 · 154	155 · Clouds
나의 가난함 · 156	157 · My poverty
아버지 제사祭祀 · 158	159 · Offerings for father
찬물 · 160	161 · Cold water
광화문 근처의 행복 · 162	163 · Happiness near Kwanghwa-mun
빛 · 166	167 · Light
술 · 168	169 · Drink
유리창 · 170	171 · Window pane
바람에게도 길이 있다 · 172	173 · The wind has paths too
구름 · 174	175 · Cloud
노래 · 176	177 · Singing

오놈 오놈 오 이쁜 놈!
You lovely fellow, you! (1987~1993)

행복 · 180	181 · *Happiness*
들국화 · 182	183 · *Wild asters*
아침 · 184	185 · *Morning*
비 · 186	187 · *Rain*
먼산山 · 188	189 · *Distant mountain*
촌놈 · 190	191 · *Country bumpkin*
꽃빛 · 192	193 · *Flower hues*
내가 좋아하는 여자 · 194	195 · *The women I like*
달 · 198	199 · *Moon*
마음 마을 · 200	201 · *Heart's village*
계곡 흐름 · 204	205 · *Flowing stream*
오월의 신록 · 206	207 · *Maytime greenery*
나의 詩作의 뜻 · 208	209 · *Notes on writing poetry*

『한국문학 영역총서』를 펴내며 · 219
Series Editor's Afterword

My Bird

피리

피리를 가졌으면 한다
달은 가지 않고
달빛은 교교히 바람만 더불고—
벌레소리도 죽은 이 밤
내 마음의 슬픈 가락에 울리어 오는
아! 피리는 어느 곳에 있는가
옛날에는
달 보신다고 다락에선 커다란 잔치
피리 부는 악관이 피리를 불면
고운 궁녀들 춤을 추었던
나도 그 피리를 가졌으면 한다
볼 수가 없다면은
만져라도 보고 싶은
이 밤
그 피리는 어느 곳에 있는가.

Flute

If only I had a flute.
The moon is unmoving
the moonlight bright alone with the wind...
tonight with all insect sounds stilled
where, alas, can that flute be
that goes so well with my heart's sad melody?
In times past
great parties were held in towers to view the moon
where the court musician would play his flute
while pretty court ladies would dance;
I wish I had that flute.
If it can't be seen, still
tonight
I long at least to touch that flute.
Where can it be?

나무

　사람들은 모두 그 나무를 썩은 나무라고 그랬다. 그러나 나는 그 나무가 썩은 나무는 아니라고 그랬다. 그 밤. 나는 꿈을 꾸었다.
　그리하여 나는 그 꿈 속에서 무럭무럭 푸른 하늘에 닿을 듯이 가지를 펴며 자라가는 그 나무를 보았다.
　나는 또다시 사람을 모아 그 나무가 썩은 나무는 아니라고 그랬다.

　그 나무는 썩은 나무가 아니다.

Tree

Everyone said that tree was rotten. But I told them that the tree was no rotten tree. That night I dreamed a dream.

In that dream I saw the tree flourishing, putting out branches as if it meant to touch the blue sky.

I called the people back again and told them that the tree was no rotten tree.

That tree is not rotten.

갈매기

그대로의 그리움이
갈매기로 하여금
구름이 되게 하였다.

기꺼운 듯
푸른 바다의 이름으로
흰 날개를 하늘에 묻어 보내어

이제 파도도
빛나는 가슴도
구름을 따라 먼 나라로 흘렀다.

그리하여 몇 번이고
몇 번이고
날아오르는 자랑이었다.

아름다운 마음이었다.

Seagull

Sheer yearning
transformed the seagull
into a cloud.

In the blue sea's name
it dyed its white wings in the sky,
evidently joyful;

then the sea,
with its so bright breast
flowed after the cloud to distant lands.

Many times
many times
it was splendor flying high.

It was a beautiful heart.

약속

한 그루의 나무도 없이
서로운 길 위에서
무엇으로 내가 서 있는가

새로운 길도 아닌
먼 길
이 길은 가도가도 황톳길인데

노을과 같이
내일과 같이
필연코 내가 무엇을 기다리고 있다.

Rendez-vous

I wonder why I'm standing
on this dreary road
where there's not a single tree?

A long road
not a new road
mile after mile of road, of red dirt road

like dusk
like tomorrow
I must be waiting for something.

갈대

환한 달빛 속에서
갈대와 나는
나란히 소리 없이 서 있었다.

불어오는 바람 속에서
안타까움을 달래며
서로 애터지게 바라보았다.

환한 달빛 속에서
갈대와 나는
눈물에 젖어 있었다.

Reed

Under the bright moonlight
a reed and I
stood side by side in silence.

Anxiously we gazed at one other
calming our distress
in the gusting wind.

In the bright moonlight
the reed and I
were both drenched with tears.

다음

멀잖아 북악에서 바람이 불고
눈을 날리며, 겨울이 온다.

그날, 눈 오는 날에
하얗게 덮인 서울의 거리를
나는 봄이 그리워서 걸어가고 있을 것이다.

아무 것도 없어도
나에게는 언제나
이러한 '다음'이 있었다.
이 새벽, 이 '다음'.
이 절대한 불가항력을
나는 내 것이라고 생각한다.

이윽고, 내일
나의 느린 걸음은
불보다도 더 뜨거운 것으로 변하여
나의 희망은
노도怒濤보다도 바다의 전부보다도
더 무거운 무게를 이 세계에 줄 것이다.

그러므로, 이 '다음'은
눈 오는 날의 서울 거리는
나의 세계의 바다로 가는 길이다.

Next

Soon the wind will blow from the northern hills
snow will fly; winter's coming.

Then on snowy days
I'll walk Seoul's snow-covered streets,
longing for spring.

Even when I had nothing at all
I always had
this "next"
this dawn, this "next".
I reckon this absolute irresistible urge
is all my own.

Soon, tomorrow,
my dragging steps transformed
into something hotter than fire
my hope
will impose on the world a heavier burden
than the surf, than all the oceans.

So this "next"
like Seoul's streets on snowy days
is the road to my world's ocean

강물

강물이 모두 바다로 흐르는 그 까닭은
언덕에 서서
내가
온종일 울었다는 그 까닭만은 아니다.

밤새
언덕에 서서
해바라기처럼 그리움에 피던
그 까닭만은 아니다.

언덕에 서서
내가
짐승처럼 서러움에 울고 있는 그 까닭은
강물이 모두 바다로만 흐르는 그 까닭만은 아니다.

River waters

The reason why the river flows toward the sea
is not only because I've been weeping
all day long
up on the hill.

Not only because I've been blooming
like a sunflower in longing
all night long
up on the hill.

The reason I've been weeping like a beast in sorrow
up on the hill
is not only because
the river flows toward the sea.

푸른 것만이 아니다

저기 저렇게 맑고 푸른 하늘을
자꾸 보고 또 보고 보는데
푸른 것만이 아니다.

외로움에 가슴 조일 때
하염없이 잎이 떨어져 오고
들에 나가 팔을 벌리면
보일 듯이 안 보일 듯이 흐르는
한 떨기 구름

3월 4월 그리고 5월의 신록
어디서 와서 달은 뜨는가
별은 밤마다 나를 보던가.

저기 저렇게 맑고 푸른 하늘을
자꾸 보고 또 보고 보는데
푸른 것만이 아니다.

Not just blue

I keep gazing gazing and gazing again
at that sky so clear and blue up there.
It's not just blue.

Sometimes I'm riven with loneliness
as petals fall unceasingly and
out in the fields as I open my arms
one cloud drifts past
now seen now unseen.

The fresh green leaves of March, April, May,
and where's the moon come rising from?
Do the stars look down at me each night?

I keep gazing, gazing
and gazing again
at that sky so clear and blue up there.
It's not just blue.

덕수궁의 오후

나뭇잎은 오후, 멀리서 한복의 여자가 손을 들어 귀를 만진다.
그 귀밑볼에 검은 혹이라도 있으면
그것은 섬돌에 떨어진 적은 꽃이파리 그늘이 된다.

구름은 떠 있다가
중화전의 파풍破風에 걸리더니 사라지고, 돌아오지 않는다

이 잔디 위와 사도砂道
다시는 못 볼 광명光明이 되어
덤덤히 섰는 솔나무에 미안한 나의 병,
내가 모르는 지나가는 사람에게 인사를 한다.

어리석음에 취하여 술도 못 마신다.
연못가로 가서 돌을 주어 물에 던지면,
끝없이 떨어져 간다.

솔나무 그늘 아래 벤치,
나는 거기로 가서 앉는다.

그러면 졸음이 와 눈을 감으면
덕수궁 전체가 돌이 되어 맑은 연못 물 속으로 떨어진다.

One afternoon in Tŏksu Palace*

A leafy afternoon; over there
a woman in traditional dress lifts a hand to her ear.
It there's even a tiny black mole on the lobe,
it turns into the shadow
of a tiny petal fallen on stone stairs.

A floating cloud meets the storm
from Chunghwa Hall, then vanishes without return.

My apologetic disease becomes a light
never again to be seen on these lawns and sandy paths
and on the dumb pines
greets passers-by I do not know.

So drunk with folly I cannot drink wine.
I go to the pond and toss in a stone;
its sinks endlessly.

I go and sit down
on a bench in the shade of the pines.

There I get drowsy and close my eyes.
The whole park is a stone sinking into a pond.

*Tŏksu Palace is in the heart of Seoul. The last king of Korea mainly lived there. The grounds are now a public park. Chunghwa Hall is the name of one of the palace's main buildings.

새

외롭게 살다 외롭게 죽을
내 영혼의 빈 터에
새날이 와, 새가 울고 꽃잎 필 때는,
내가 죽는 날
그 다음날.

산다는 것과
아름다운 것과
사랑한다는 것과의 노래가
한창인 때에
나는 도랑과 나뭇가지에 앉은
한 마리 새.

정감에 그득찬 계절,
슬픔과 기쁨의 주일,
알고 모르고 잊고 하는 사이에
새여 너는
낡은 목청을 뽑아라.

살아서
좋은 일도 있었다고
나쁜 일도 있었다고
그렇게 우는 한 마리 새.

Bird

The day beyond
the day I die
lonely in death after lonely living
birds will sing as new day dawns and petals unfold
on my soul's empty ground.

I'll be one bird
alighting on ditches and branches
when the song of loving
and living
and beauty
is at its height.

Season full of emotion
week of sorrow and joy
in the gaps between knowing, not knowing, forgetting
bird
pour out that antiquated song.

One bird sings of how
there are good things
in life
and bad things too.

새 2

그러노라고
뭐라고, 하루를 지껄이다가,
잠잔다 -

바다의 침묵, 나는 잠잔다.
아들이 늙은 아버지 편지를 받듯이
꿈으로 꾼다.

바로 그날 하루에 말한 모든 말들이,
이미 죽은 사람들의 외마디 소리와
서로 안으며, 사랑했던 것이나 아니었을까?
그 꿈속에서……

하루의 언어를 위해, 나는 노래한다.
나의 노래여, 나의 노래여,
슬픔을 대신하여, 나의 노래는 밤에 잠잔다.

Bird 2

After chattering all day long
saying things
now I fall asleep...

Sea silent, I fall asleep
and dream dreams
like the letters a son gets from an aged father.

All the words I said today
seem to be embracing and making love
to the screams of those already dead.
In those dreams, I mean...

I sing for each day's spoken words.
Ah, my song, my song!
At night, instead of sorrow, my song falls asleep.

새 3

저 새는 날지 않고 울지 않고
내내 움직일 줄 모른다.
상처가 매우 깊은 모양이다.
아시지의 성聖프란시스코는
새들에게
은총 설교를 했다지만
저 새는 그저 아프기만 한 모양이다.
수백 년 전 그날 그 벌판의 일몰日沒과 백야白夜는
오늘 이 땅 위에
눈을 내리게 하는데
눈이 내리는데……

Bird 3

That bird can't fly or sing
it can't even move.
It must be deeply wounded.
St Francis of Assissi preached
of grace
to the birds
but that bird seems just as sick as before.
The sunset and dusk on the fields long centuries ago
are making snow fall
here today.
It's snowing...

주막에서

―도끼가 내 목을 찍은 그 훨씬 전에 내 안에서 죽어간 즐거운 아기들 (장 주네)

골목에서 골목으로
거기 조그만 주막집.
할머니 한 잔 더 주세요,
저녁 어스름은 가난한 시인의 보람인 것을……
흐리멍텅한 눈에 이 세상은 다만
순하기 순하기 마련인가,
할머니 한 잔 더 주세요.
몽롱하다는 것은 장엄하다.
골목 어귀에서 서툰 걸음인 양
밤은 깊어 가는데,
할머니 등 뒤에
고향의 뒷산이 솟고
그 산에는
철도 아닌 한겨울의 눈이 평평 쏟아지고 있는 것이다.
그 산너머
쓸쓸한 성황당 꼭대기,
그 꼭대기 위에서
함박 눈을 맞으며, 아기들이 놀고 있다.
아기들은 매우 즐거운 모양이다.
한없이 즐거운 모양이다.

In a tavern

–For the happy child that died within me long before the blade fell on my neck (Jean Genet)

From alleyway to alleyway
and now in this tiny tavern.
Pour me one more glass, old dear.
Evening dusk's a poor poet's reward...
Is it normal, I wonder, for this world to appear
as smooth as it does to troubled eyes?
Pour me one more glass, old dear.
Hazy things are solemn.
At the entry to the alley
the night is growing darker with awkward steps
but behind the old woman's back
looms the hill beside my home village
and on that hill
unseasonable winter snow is falling heavily.
Beyond that hill,
on the lonely ridge with the local god's shrine
above that ridge,
hurling lumps of soft snow, the kids are playing.
The children are looking very cheerful.
They look infinitely cheerful.

새

저것 앞에서는
눈이란 다만 무력할 따름
가을 하늘가에 길게 뻗친 가지 끝에,
점찍힌 저 절대 정지를 보겠다면……

본다는 것은 무엇인가
있는 것과 없는 것의
미묘하기 그지없는 간격을,
이어주는 다리橋는 무슨 상형象形인가.

저것은
무너진 시계視界 위에 슬며시 깃을 펴고
핏빛깔의 햇살을 쪼으며
불현 듯이 왔다 사라지지 않는가.

바람은 소리 없이 이는데
이 하늘, 저 하늘의
순수균형을
그토록 간신히 지탱하는 새 한 마리.

Bird

Before it
eyes are quite useless
in the effort to see the utter stillness imprinted
on the tip of branches long against the autumn sky...

What is meant by seeing?
What form can the bridge have that spans
the infinitely subtle difference
between what is and what is not?

Won't that thing
that pecks at blood-tinged sunbeams
gently spreading feathers over ruined visions
vanish as suddenly as it came?

So as the wind blows soundlessly
one bird is barely maintaining
the perfect balance
between this sky and that.

곡哭 신동엽

어느 구름 개인 날
어쩌다 하늘이
그 옆얼굴을 내어보일 때,

그 맑은 눈
한곬으로 쏠리는 곳
네 무덤 있거라.

잡초 무더기.
저만치 가장자리에
꽃, 그 외로움을 자랑하듯,

신동엽!
꼭 너는 그런 사내였다.

아무리 잠깐이라지만
그 잠깐만 두어두고
너는 갔다.

저쪽 저
영광의 나라로!

Lament for Shin Dong–yŏp*

On a cloudless day
the sky revealed itself
from time to time in profile.

Its one clear eye
steadily gazing down
was fixed on your tomb.

At the farthest limit
of the grassy mound
a flower grew, boasting of its solitude.

Shin Dong–yŏp!
That's the kind of man you were.

No matter for how short a moment
you left everything there
and off you went.

Off away
to the land of glory!

*The poet Shin Dong–yŏp was one of Ch'ŏn Sang Pyŏng's contemporaries. Born in 1930 in Puyo, he died in 1969. His work is marked by a strong concern with social questions. His most noted work is the long poetic cycle Kŭm-gang.

주일 1

오늘같이 맑은 가을 하늘 위
그 한층 더 위에 구름이 흐릅니다.

성당 입구 바로 앞
저는 지금 기다리고 있습니다.

입구 지키는 교통순경이
닦기 끝나면 저도 닦으려고요.

교통순경의 그 마음가짐보다
저가 못한데서야 말이 아닙니다.

오늘같이 맑은 가을 하늘 위
그 한층 더 위에 구름이 흐릅니다.

Sabbath 1

Above autumn skies as bright as today's
one flight above, a cloud goes drifting.

Here I am at present waiting
right in front of the church gate

to have my shoes shined after the policeman
on traffic duty at the gate.

It would be a pity if I were less considerate
than that policeman.

Above autumn skies as bright as today's
one flight above, a cloud goes drifting.

주일 2

1
그는 걷고 있었습니다.
골목에서 거리로,
옆길에서 큰길로,

즐비하게 늘어선
상점과 건물이 있습니다.
상관 않고 그는 걷고 있었습니다.

어디까지 가겠느냐구요?
숲으로, 바다로,
별을 향하여
그는 쉬지 않고 걷고 있습니다.

2
낮에는 찻집, 술집으로
밤에는 여인숙.

나의 길은
언제나 꼭 같았는데……

그러나
오늘은 딴 길을 간다.

Sabbath 2

1

He went walking on.
From alley to street
from side-street to main road.

Stores and buildings
lined up side by side in rows.
Heedless he went walking on.

How far is he going, you ask?
To the woods, to the sea.
Heading for the stars
unresting he goes walking on.

2

By day to a teashop, or a bar,
at night to an inn.

My paths
always used to be the same...

Yet
today I'm taking another path.

회상 1

아름다워라, 젊은 날 사랑의 대꾸는
어딜 가?
어딜 가긴 어딜 가요?

아름다워라, 젊은 날 사랑의 대꾸는
널 사랑해!
그래도 난 죽어도 싫어요!

눈 오는 날 사랑은 쌓인다.
비 오는 날 세월은 흐른다.

Memories 1

How beautiful the rejoinders of youthful love.
Where shall we go?
Nowhere special. Why?

How beautiful the rejoinders of youthful love.
I love you!
I hate you, no matter what you say!

On snowy days love drifts.
On rainy days time flows.

편지

점심을 얻어먹고 배부른 내가
배고팠던 나에게 편지를 쓴다.

옛날에도 더러 있었던 일,
그다지 섭섭하진 않겠지?

때론 호사로운 적도 없지 않았다.
그걸 잊지 말아주기 바란다.

내일을 믿다가
이십 년!

배부른 내가
그걸 잊을까 걱정이 되어서

나는
자네한테 편지를 쓴다네.

Letter

With my stomach full after eating lunch
I'm writing this letter to the once hungry me.

It used to happen sometimes.
You won't be upset, will you?

There were times of luxury too, you know.
I hope you won't forget that.

I was sure of tomorrow
for twenty years!

Now that I'm full
I'm worried I might forget all that

so I'm
writing this letter.

진혼가

　　－저쪽 죽음의 섬에는 내 청춘의 무덤도 있다(니체)

태고적 고요가
바다를 딛고 있는
그 곳.

안개 자욱이
석유불처럼 흐르는
그 곳.

인적 없고
후미진
그 곳.

새 무덤,
물결에 씻긴다.

Requiem

—In yonder isle of death is also the tomb of my youth (Nietsche)

A place
where ancient stillness
walks the sea.

A place
where mists flow thick
like oil ablaze.

A secluded
uninhabited
place.

A fresh grave
washed by the waves.

국화꽃

오늘만의 밤은 없었어도
달은 떴고
별은 반짝였다.

괴로움만의 날은 없어도
해는 다시 떠오르고
아침은 열렸다.

무심만이 내가 아니라도
탁자 위 컵에 꽂힌
한 송이 국화꽃으로
나는 빛난다!

One chrysanthemum

Although for today there was no night
the moon came up
the stars were twinkling bright.

Although there's no day with only grief
once again the sun rose
the morning dawned.

I'm not utter innocence
but thanks to that one chrysanthemum
standing in a cup on the table
I'm all aglow.

회상 2

그 길을 다시 가면
봄이 오고,

고개를 넘으면
여름빛 쬐인다.

돌아오는 길에는
가을이 낙엽 흩날리게 하고,

겨울은 별 수 없이
함박눈 쏟아진다.

내가 네게 쓴
사랑의 편지.

그 사랑의 글자에는
그러한 뜻이, 큰 강물 되어 도도히 흐른다.

Memories 2

If I go that way again
spring comes

If I pass beyond the hill
summer light shines.

On the way back
autumn leaves are drifting

and winter inevitably
scatters great flakes of snow.

The love letters
I wrote to you

the writings of love
have likewise turned into great rivers flowing vast.

아가야

    해 뜨기 전 새벽 중간쯤 희부연 어스름을 타고 낙심을 이리처럼 깨물며, 사직공원 길을 간다. 행인도 드문 이 거리 어느 집 문 밖에서 서너 살 됨직한 잠옷바람의 애띤 계집애가 울고 있다. 지겹도록 슬피 운다. 지겹도록 슬피 운다. 웬일일까? 개와 큰집 대문 밖에서 유리 같은 손으로 문을 두드리며 이 애기는 왜 울고 있을까? 오줌이나 싼 그런 벌을 받고 있는 걸까? 자주 뒤돌아보면서 나는 무심할 수가 없었다.
    아가야, 왜 우니? 이 인생의 무엇을 안다고 우니? 무슨 슬픔 당했다고, 괴로움이 얼마나 아픈가를 깨쳤다고 우니? 이 새벽 정처없는 산길로 헤매어 가는 이 아저씨도 울지 않는데……
    아가야, 너에게는 그 문을 곧 열어줄 엄마손이 있겠지. 이 아저씨에게는 그런 사랑이 열릴 문도 없단다. 아가야 울지마! 이런 아저씨도 울지 않는데……

Little child

In the early hours before sunrise, taking the wings of the pale grey dawn, I set off for Sajik Park*, gnawing dejection as I went. Down an almost deserted street a little girl, only three or four, was standing crying outside one house's front gate, dressed in her nightclothes. She was sobbing dreadfully, sobbing dreadfully. I wonder why?

Why is this little child crying here outside this big house's front door, complete with its guard-dog, pressing the gate with her glass-like hand? Perhaps she's being punished for wetting her bed? All the time looking back, I cannot ignore her.

Little girl, why are you crying? Because you've just learned something about life? Because something sad has happened, and you've experienced how very much painful things hurt? Yet this fellow here, aimlessly wandering up the hill in the dawn, isn't crying...

Little girl, you've got a mother whose hand's soon going to open that gate for sure. This fellow here has no door for any such love to open. Don't cry, little child! After all, look at me: I'm not crying...

---

*Sajik Park lies a few hundred yards to the west of the old royal palace of Kyŏngbok-gung. It is the site of the altar where the kings of Korea used to celebrate offerings to the Earth spirits. It is now a public park.

음악

이것은 무슨 음악이지요? 새벽녘 머리맡에 와서 속삭이는 그 윽한 소리. 눈물 뿌리며 옛날에 듣던 이 곡의 작곡가는 평생 한 여자를 사랑하다 갔지요? 아마 그 여자의 이름은 클라라일 겝니다. 그의 스승의 아내였지요? 백 년 이백 년 세월은 흘러도 그의 사랑은 아직 다하지 못한 모양입니다. 그래서 오늘 새벽녘 멀고 먼 나라 엉망진창인 이 파락호의 가슴에까지 와서 울고 있지요?

Music

What kind of music is this? A quiet whisper close beside my pillow in the early hours. I think the composer of this tune, that I used to listen to with tears, loved one girl his whole life long. It may be that her name was Clara. Wasn't she his teacher's wife? One century, two centuries of time have rolled by and yet it looks as though his love is still not over. Early this morning it's come to the heart of this messed-up wreck living in a distant land and weeps.

귀천

나 하늘로 돌아가리라
새벽빛 와 닿으면 스러지는
이슬 더불어 손에 손을 잡고,

나 하늘로 돌아가리라.
노을빛 함께 단둘이서
기슭에서 놀다가 구름 손짓하며는,

나 하늘로 돌아가리라.
아름다운 이 세상 소풍 끝내는 날,
가서, 아름다웠더라고 말하리라……

Back to Heaven*

I'll go back to heaven again.
Hand in hand with the dew
that melts at a touch of the dawning day,

I'll go back to heaven again.
With the dusk, together, just we two,
at a sign from a cloud after playing on the slopes

I'll go back to heaven again.
At the end of my outing to this beautiful world
I'll go back and say: It was beautiful...

---

*The title of this poem, the Chinese characters Kwi(return) and Ch'ŏn(Heaven), gave its name to the tiny café in Seoul's Insadong neighborhood run by Mok Sun Ok, the poet's wife. ("The smallest café in the world", the poet claims in a poem not included in this selection.)

This is the poet's best-known poem, it has several times been set to music.

들국화

산등성 외따른 데,
애기 들국화.

바람도 없는데
괜히 몸을 뒤뉘인다.

가을은
다시 올 테지.

다시 올까?
나와 네 외로운 마음이,
지금처럼
순하게 겹친 이 순간이……

Daisies

A lonely spot on a hilltop ridge
with tiny daisies.

There's no wind,
yet somehow they're fluttering.

Autumn
will come again.

Will this moment come again?
My lonely heart and yours
chastely united
as now...

한낮의 별빛

돌담 가까이
창가에 흰 빨래들
지붕 가까이
애기처럼 고이 잠든
한낮의 별빛을 너는 보느냐……

슬픔 옆에서
지겨운 기다림
사랑의 몸짓 옆에서
맴도는 저 세상 같은
한낮의 별빛을 너는 보느냐……

물결 위에서
바윗덩이 위에서
사막 위에서
극으로 달리는
한낮의 별빛을 너는 보느냐……

새는
온갖 한낮의 별빛 계곡을 횡단하면서
울고 있다.

Daytime starlight

Do you see the daytime starlight
sleeping quietly like a baby
near the roof
the white clothes hanging by the window
near the garden wall...

Do you see the daytime starlight
like that spinning world
beside love's gestures
the wearisome waiting
alongside of sorrow...

Do you see the daytime starlight
speeding pole-wards
over deserts
over rocks
over waves...

A bird
traverses all the daytime starlight valleys
singing.

"크레이지 배가본드"

1
오늘의 바람은 가고
내일의 바람이 불기 시작한다.

잘 가거라
오늘은 너무 시시하다.

뒷시궁창 쥐새끼 소리같이
내일의 바람이 불기 시작한다.

2
하늘을 안고,
바다를 품고,
한 모금 담배를 빤다.

하늘을 안고,
바다를 품고,
한 모금 물을 마신다.

누군가 앉았다 간 자리
우물가, 꽁초 토막……

"Crazy Vagabond"

1

Today's wind is leaving
tomorrow's wind is beginning to blow.

Bye-bye.
Today's been far too dull.

Like baby rats mewling in a backyard cesspit
tomorrow's wind is beginning to blow.

2

Hugging the sky
embracing the sea
I draw on a cigarette.

Hugging the sky
embracing the sea
I drink a draught of water.

Someone sat for a while beside the well
then went on, leaving a fag-end behind...

미소

－새

1
입가 흐뭇스레 진 엷은 웃음은,
삶과 죽음 가에 살짝 걸린
실오라기 외나무다리.

새는 그 다리 위를 날아간다.
우정과 결심, 그리고 용기
그런 양 나래 저으며……

풀잎 슬몃 건드리는 바람이기보다
그 뿌리에 와 닿아주는 바람,
이 가슴팍에서 빛나는 햇발.

오늘도 가고 내일도 갈
풀밭 길에서
입가 언덕에 맑은 웃음 몇 번인가는……

2
햇빛 반짝이는 언덕으로 오라
나의 친구여,

언덕에서 언덕으로 가기에는
수많은 바다를 건너야 한다지만,

햇빛 반짝이는 언덕으로 오라
나의 친구여……

Smile

–Bird

1

This thin smile lurking smug on my lips
is a bridge composed of a single thread
deftly slung at the brink of life and death.

A bird goes flying up that bridge.
Fraternity and resolution with courage too
wafting on just such pinions...

Not a breeze furtively shaking the leaves
but rather a wind that touches the roots
the sunbeams streaming from this breast.

How often will my lips smile bright at the hills
along the meadow path
taken today, and tomorrow too...

2

My friend
come to this sun-shimmering hill.

Though you have to cross many oceans
to pass from hill to hill, still

come to this sun-shimmering hill
my friend...

나의 가난은

오늘 아침을 다소 행복하다고 생각는 것은
한 잔 커피와 갑 속의 두둑한 담배,
해장을 하고도 버스값이 남았다는 것.

오늘 아침을 다소 서럽다고 생각는 것은
잔돈 몇 푼에 조금도 부족이 없어도
내일 아침 일도 걱정해야 하기 때문이다.

가난은 내 직업이지만
비쳐오는 이 햇빛에 떳떳할 수가 있는 것은
이 햇빛에도 예금통장은 없을 테니까……

나의 과거와 미래
사랑하는 내 아들딸들아,
내 무덤가 무성한 풀섶으로 때론 와서
괴로웠을 그런대로 산 인생. 여기 잠들다. 라고,
씽씽 바람 불어라……

My poverty

I feel fairly happy this morning,
with a cup of coffee, enough fags in the pack,
one for the road and still the bus fare left over.

I feel fairly gloomy this morning,
though I'm not short of small change,
because I have to worry about tomorrow.

Poverty's my full-time job
but if I can hold up my head in this sunshine
it's because the sunshine has no bank account either.

My past and future
my dear sons and daughters,
sometimes come to my grass-grown grave and say,
here sleeps a life that took pain in its stride,
let the fresh breeze blow...

간의 반란

육십 먹은 노인과 마주 앉았다.
걱정할 거 없네,
그러면 어쩌지요?
될 대로 될 걸세……

보지도 못한 내 간이
괘씸하게도 쿠데타를 일으켰다.
그 쪼무래기가 뭘 할까만은
아직도 살고픈 목숨 가까이 다가온다.

나는 원래 쿠데타를 좋아하지 않는다.
그 수습을
늙은 의사에게 묻는데,
대책이라고는 시간 따름인가!

Liver revolt

I sat facing a sixty-year old man.
Don't worry. Relax.
But still, what must I do?
We'll just have to wait and see...

My completely unseen liver
has dared to stage a coup d'état.
There's not much that little fellow can do
yet a life still eager to live comes home to me.

I don't much like coup d'états.
I ask the old doctor
how to deal with it.
Policies depend on situations!

넋

넋이 있느냐 라는 것은,
내가 있느냐 없느냐고 묻는 거나 같다.
산을 보면서 산이 없다고 하겠느냐?
나의 넋이여!
마음껏 발동해 다오.
내 몸의 모든 움직임은,
바로 내 넋의 가면이다.
비 오는 날 내가 다소 우울해지면,
그것은 즉 넋이 우울하다는 것이다.
내 넋을 전세계로 해방하여
내 넋을 넓직하게 발동케 하고 싶다.

Soul

Asking if I have a soul
is like asking if I exist or not.
Can you see a hill and say it's not there?
My soul!
Run wild.
My body's movements
are my soul's disguise, that's all.
When I'm gloomy on rainy days,
it's my soul that's gloomy.
I want my soul to be free worldwide,
able to run all over the place.

한 가지 소원

나의 다소 명석한 지성과 깨끗한 영혼이
흙 속에 묻혀 살과 같이
문드러지고 진물이 나 삭여진다고?

야스퍼스는
과학에게 그 자체의 의미를 물어도
절대로 대답하지 못한다고 했는데-

억지밖에 없는 엽전 세상에서
용케도 이때껏 살았나 싶다.
별다른 불만은 없지만,

똥걸레 같은 지성은 썩어 버려도
이런 시를 쓰게 하는 내 영혼은
어떻게 좀 안 될지 모르겠다.

내가 죽은 여러 해 뒤에는
꾹 쥔 십 원을 슬쩍 주고는
서울길 밤버스를 내 영혼은 타고 있지 않을까?

One Wish

You think my fairly lucid mind and my spotless soul,
buried together with my flesh in the ground,
will also rot and ooze and be devoured?

Jaspers said
that if you ask science about its own significance,
it is utterly unable to reply.

In this halfpenny world of utter obstinacy
I wonder how I have managed to survive at all.
I've no particular complaint to make

but though my shitty mind may rot
it's altogether another matter when it comes
to the soul that's making me write this poem.

Years after I die, maybe my soul
will be boarding late buses in the streets of Seoul,
gladly paying the penny it's been clutching so hard.

만추晩秋
―주일主日

내년 이 꽃을 이을 씨앗은
바람 속에 덧없이 뛰어들어 가지고,
핏발 선 눈길로 행방을 찾는다.

숲에서 숲으로, 산에서 산으로,
무전여행을 하다가
모래사장에서 목말라 혼이 난다.

어린 양 한 마리 돌아오다.
땅을 말없이 다정하게 맞으며,
안락의 집으로 안내한다.

마리아.
나에게도 이 꽃의 일생을 주십시오.

Late Autumn

–Sunday

A seed that will be this flower next year
has plunged fleetingly into the breeze
seeking its way with bloodshot eyes.

After wandering penniless
from wood to wood, hill to hill,
it has to endure agonies of thirst in a sandbank.

At last a little lamb comes home.
Tenderly meeting the ground without a word
it is guided to the house of rest.

Mary!
Grant me a lifetime like this flower.

소릉조小陵調
-70년 추석에

아버지 어머니는
고향 산소에 있고

외톨배기 나는
서울에 있고

형과 누이들은
부산에 있는데,

여비가 없으니
가지 못한다.

저승 가는 데도
여비가 든다면

나는 영영
가지도 못하나?

생각느니, 아,
인생은 얼마나 깊은 것인가.

A La Tu Fu

—Ch'usok, 1970

Father and mother lie
in the family burial plot at home

I'm all on my own
here in Seoul

brother and sisters
are down in Pusan

but I don't have the fare
so I can't go.

If there's a fare to pay
when you pass away

does that mean
I'll never be able to go?

When you think of it, ah,
what a deep thing life is.

그날은

  -새

이젠 몇 년이었는가
아이론 및 와이셔츠같이
당한 그날은……

이젠 몇 년이었는가
무서운 집 뒷창가에 여름 곤충 한 마리
땀 흘리는 나에게 악수를 청한 그날은……

내 살과 뼈는 알고 있다.
진실과 고통
그 어느 쪽이 강자인가를……

내 마음 하늘
한편 가에서
새는 소스라치게 날개 편다.

That day

–Bird

That day, when I suffered
like a shirt beneath the iron,
I can't say how many years ago...

That day when one summer bug tried to shake hands with me
as I perspired by a back window in a fearful house
I can't say how many years ago...

Your flesh and bones all know
which is mightier,
sincerity or pain...

To one side
of the heaven in my mind
a bird is stretching its wings in alarm.

꽃의 위치에 대하여

꽃이 하등 이런 꼬락서니로 필게 뭐람
아름답기 짝이 없고 상냥하고 소리 없고
영 터무니없이 초대인적超大人的이기도 하구나.

현명한 인간도 웬만큼 해서는 당하지 못하리니······
어떤 절색황후께서도 되려 부끄러워했을 것이다.
이런 이름 짓기가 더러 있었지 않는가 싶다.

미스터 유니버시티일지라도 우락부락해도······
과연 이 꽃송이를 함부로 꺾을 수가 있을까······
한다는 수작이 그 찬송가가 아니었을까······

The place of flowers

What makes flowers bloom like this?
Beautiful beyond compare, tender and so quiet,
they're quite preposterously superhuman.

Even our wisest doing their best can't rival them...
Try as she may, the fairest princess is bound to fail.
There are sometimes things like this to name.

Not even Mr University, no matter how rugged...
How could anyone roughly pluck this flower...
Wasn't he singing a hymn, foolishly at that...

광화문에서

 아침길 광화문에서 <눈물의 여왕> 그녀의 장례 행진을 본다. 만장이 나부끼고, 악대가 붕붕거리고, 여러 대의 차와 군중이 길을 메웠다. 나는 곰곰이 생각해 보았다. 죽은 내 아버지도 <눈물의 여왕> 그녀의 열렬한 팬이었댔지…… 아니다. 그런 것이 아니다. 문인들 장례식도 예총광장에서 더러 있었다. 만장도 없고, 악대는커녕, 행진은커녕 아주 형편없는, 초라하기 짝이 없는 모임이었다. 그 초라함을 위해서만이 그들은 <시>를 썼다.

At Kwanghwa–mun*

Out early at Kwanghwa–mun, I witnessed the funeral procession of the star they called "The Queen of Tears." The funeral banners were streaming, the band was tootling, while several buses and a great crowd filled the road. I mused thoughtfully. About how my late father had been a devoted fan of that same Queen of Tears...? No, not that. How sometimes the funerals of writers have passed the same way. With no banners, certainly no band, and absolutely no procession, a totally wretched, incomparably seedy-looking gathering. To earn that seediness was the sole reason they wrote poetry.

---

*Kwanghwa–mun is the name of the main gateway to the royal palace, Kyŏngbok-gung, in the center of Seoul, and by extension the name of the road and of the major intersection a few hundred yards in front of it.

주막에서

In a tavern

눈

고요한데 잎사귀가 날아와서
네 가슴에 떨어져 간다.

떨어진 자리는
오목하게 파인

그 순간 앗 할 사이도 없이
네 목숨을 내보내게 한
상처 바로 옆이다.

거기서 잎사귀는
지금 일심으로
네 목숨을 들여다보며 너를 본다

자꾸 바람이 불어오고
또 불어오는데
꼼짝 않고 상처를 지키는 잎사귀

그 잎사귀는 눈이다 눈이다
맑은 하늘의 눈 우리들의 눈 분노의
너를 부르는 어머니의 눈물어린 눈이다

Eyes

Silently a leaf comes fluttering down
drops on my chest and is gone.

The spot where it falls
is just beside the wound

deeply scored
that drove me out into life
with not a moment then to utter a cry.

There the leaf
is now wholeheartedly
watching you as it examines your life.

The wind keeps on blowing
on and on blowing
the leaf watching motionless over the wound

That leaf is an eye, an eye,
clear heaven's eye, our eye, mother's
angry tearful eye as she calls you.

내 집

누가 나에게 집을 사 주지 않겠는가? 하늘을 우러러 목터지게 외친다. 들려다오 세계가 끝날 때까지 …… 나는 결혼식을 몇 주 전에 마쳤으니 어찌 이렇게 부르짖지 못하겠는가? 천상의 하나님은 미소로 들을 게다. 불란서의 아르투르랭보 시인은 영국의 런던에서 짤막한 신문광고를 냈다. 누가 나를 남쪽 나라로 데려가지 않겠는가. 어떤 선장이 이것을 보고, 쾌히 상선에 실어 남쪽 나라로 실어 주었다. 그러니 거인처럼 부르짖는다. 집은 보물이다. 전세계가 허물어져도 내 집은 남겠다……

My house

Won't somebody give me a house? I roar to the heavens. Hear me, someone, to the ends of the earth... I got married just a few weeks ago, so how can I help but shout like this? God in his heaven will hear with a smile. The French poet Arthur Rimbaud put an ad in a London newspaper. "Won't someone take me to a southern country?" A ship's captain saw it, gladly took him on board and shipped him to a southern country. So I'm shouting like a giant. A house is a treasure. The whole world may crumble and fall, my house will remain.

비 7

8월 장마비는 늦은뱅이다.
농사에는 알맞아 들 테지마는,
인간에겐 하찮은 쓰레기일 것이니……

먼 데 제주도 생각이 불현 듯 나니……
아직 한 번도 못 가본 제주도여,
마치 런던 옆에나 있는 것이 아니냐.

애오라지 못 갈 바에야,
바닷가로나 가서 먼 데까지 가야지……
그러면은 그 섬 향기가 날지도 모른다.

Rain 7

The monsoons are late in coming.
They were needed for the crops
but that's all junk for ordinary folks...

I suddenly think of remote Cheju Island*...
I was never once able to visit it!
Isn't it somewhere near London?

There's no way I'll ever get there.
I must make a long journey, to the coast at least...
Then the scent of that island may come drifting by.

---

*Cheju Island is a large island off the south-west coast of Korea.

비 8

백두산 천지에는
언제나 비가 쏟아진다드냐……
단군 할아버지께서 우산을 쓰셨겠다.

압록강의 원류가 큰소리를 칠 것이니
정암頂岩이 소용돌이 쳐
범조차 그 공포에 흐늘흐늘일 것이다.

백운白雲을 읊는 고전시는 있어도,
이 산을 읊는 고전시는 없었다.
그러니 내가 읊는 수밖에 없지 않느냐.

Rain 8

Is rain really always pouring down
into Ch'ŏnji Lake on Paektu Mountain*?
Old Father Tangun must have used an umbrella.

The falls at the head of the Yalu River roar down
and form such a great whirlpool
that even the tiger has to tremble for fear.

There may be a classical poem about white clouds,
there's no classical poem about this mountain.
So I'm obliged to write one, I suppose?

**Mount Paektu is an extinct volcano on the Korean-Chinese border; in its crater there is a large lake, called Ch'ŏnji in Korean, fed by almost constant rain. The lake empties through a famous waterfall to give birth to the great Yalu River that flows westward to form the main frontier with China.*

Old Father Tangun is the mythical founder of the Korean nation. He is said to have been born in 2223 B.C., the offspring of a heavenly visitor and a bear transformed into a woman. There are legends associating him with various mountain peaks, including that of Mount Paektu.

비 11

빗물은 대단히 순진무구하다.
하루만 비가 와도,
어제의 말랐던 계곡물이 불어 오른다.

죽은 김관식은
사람은 강가에 산다고 했는데,
보아하니 그게 진리대왕이다.

나무는 왜 강가에 무성한가
물을 찾아서가 아니고
강가의 정취를 기어코 사랑하기 때문이다.

Rain 11

Rain is extremely pure and innocent.
Even if it only rains for a day
the mountain streams, that were dry before, swell.

The late poet Kim Kwan-sik*
used to say that humans live at riversides;
by the looks of it that's the king of truths.

Why do trees grow so luxuriantly at riversides?
Not because they've got enough water there
but because they love the riverside mood.

---

*Kim Kwan-sik (1934~1970) was a poet, and a friend of Ch'ŏn Sang Pyŏng.

비

1
저 구름의 연연連連한 부피는
온 하늘을 암흑대륙으로 싸았으니
괴묵怪默은 그냥, 비만 내리니 천만다행이다.
지금 장마철이니

저 암흑대륙에 저 만리장성이다.
우레소리 또한 있을 만하지 않은가.

우주야말로 신비경이 아니냐?
달과 별은 한낮엔 어디로 갔단 말이냐?
비는 그 청신호인지 모르지 않느냐?

2
새벽같이 올라와야 했던
이 약수는
몇 월 며칠의 빗물인지도 모르겠다.

산과 옆의 바다는 알 터이나,
하늘과 구름은 뻔히 알겠지만,
입이 없으니, 안타까울 따름이다.

Rain

1

Like a dark continent, an uninterrupted mass
of clouds is covering the sky
in a strange silence, luckily it's raining.
It's the rainy season now

and on that dark continent lies the Great Wall.
Perhaps there may be peals of thunder.

Isn't the universe a land of mystery?
Where do the moon and stars go in the daytime?
Maybe rain's the green light for them?

2

This spring water
obliged to rise now with the dawn
was perhaps rain that fell on such and such a day.

The hill itself and the nearby rocks may know,
the sky and clouds must know for sure
but they have no mouths, it's frustrating.

이 약수를 마시는 데는 지장이 없고,
맛이 달라질 수는 없을 것이니
재수형통만 빌 뿐이다.

3
상식적으로 비는 삼라만상 위에 내린다.
그런데 지붕뿐인 줄 알고,
내실의 꽃병은 아니 맞는 줄 안다.

생각해 보라
삼라만상은 이 우주의 전부이다.
그러니 그 꽃병도 한참 맞고 있는 것이다.

생리는 그 꽃병을 안 맞게 하지만
실존은 그 꽃병의 진짜 정신을
지붕 위에 있게 하여 비를 맞는 것이다.

4
물의 원소는
수소 두 개와 산소이지만
벌써 중학생 때 익히 알았다.

그런데 알 수 없는 것은
그 수소와 산소 뒤에는

There's no harm in drinking this spring-water,
it's taste can never vary,
you only need pray for good luck.

3

From a commonsensical view, rain falls on all of Nature.
But you think it's just falling on the roof
not realizing it's striking the vase inside.

Only think!
Nature's the whole of the cosmos.
Which is why it's striking the vase as well.

Physically the vase is not being struck
but in actual fact the vase's real soul,
being raised to the roof, is getting rained on.

4

The chemical composition of water
is two hydrogen atoms and one oxygen
I already knew that in middle school.

But I still don't know
what on earth there is

도대체 무엇이 들어 있단 말인가……

공포할 만한 야수가 들어 있다.
수소 뒤에는 수소폭탄이,
산소 뒤에는 원자폭탄이……

5
나는 국민학교 때는
비가 오기만 하면
학교엘 가지 아니하였다.

이제는 천국에 가신 어머니에게
한사코 콩을 볶아달라고 하여
몸이 아프다고 핑계했었다.

이제는 나가겠으나
이미 나이가 사십이니
이 세계를 거꾸로 한들 소용이 없다.

behind that hydrogen and oxygen...

What's in there is a wild beast fit to be feared.
A hydrogen bomb behind the hydrogen
an atom bomb behind the oxygen...

5
When I was in primary school
if ever it rained
I didn't use to go to school.

I would desperately beg my mother
(she's already gone to the kingdom of heaven)
to bake me some beans because I was sick.

I'll go out now
but seeing I'm already forty
it's no use setting the world back to front.

봄소식

입춘이 지나니 훨씬 덜 춥구나!
겨울이 아니고 봄 같으니,
달력을 아래 위로 쳐다보기만 한다.

새로운 입김이며
그건 대지의 작란作亂인가!
꽃들도 이윽고 만발하리라.

아슴푸레히 반짝이는 태양이여.
왜 그렇게도 외로운가.
북극이 온지대溫地帶가 될 게 아닌가.

News of spring

Ipch'un's * come, it's much less cold!
Winter's over, spring's nearly here.
I scan the calendar up and down.

Steaming breath again?
Earth's idea of a joke!
Soon flowers will be blooming.

Faintly gleaming sun,
why are you so gloomy?
Won't the arctic turn into the tropics?

*Ipch'un (onset of spring) is the name given to a day in early February, the date varying slightly from year to year. It is one of the twenty-four "seasonal" dates superimposed on the traditional lunar calendar.

8월의 종소리

저 소리는 무슨 소리일까?
땅의 소리인가?
하늘 소리인가?

한참 생각하니, 종소리.
멀리 멀리서 들리는 소리.

저 소리는 어디까지 갈까?
우주 끝까지 갈지도 모른다.
땅속까지 스밀 것이고,
천국에서도 들릴 것인가?

August bell

What can that sound be?
The sound of the earth?
The sound of the sky?

A moment's thought: the sound of a bell
a sound heard from far far away.

How far will that sound go?
Maybe to the ends of space.
Or perhaps it will sink beneath the ground
and even be heard in the kingdom of heaven?

시냇물가 5

시냇물이 세차게 흘러가며
심지어 파도를 쳤다.
바위에 부딪쳐, 물결이 거세게 화를 냈다.

어제와 지난 밤에 비가 억수로 왔으니
산에 내린 물이 소나무 밑으로 헤매다가
드디어 계곡에 집합하여 이 꼴이다.

산세와 지세가 바다보다 높아서
자연히 밑으로 물이 흐를 수밖에,
그렇지만 오늘같이 노도怒濤를 치는 것은 처음이다.

Streamside 5

As the stream poured fiercely down
it even broke into waves.
Striking rocks, its billows raged in fury.

It poured yesterday all day and all night until
the water falling in the hills, wandering beneath the pines
united in the valley in this shape.

Hills and land being physically higher than the sea
water is naturally bound to flow downwards
but today's the first time I ever saw waves raging so.

인생서가 人生序歌

격언은 진리 이상이야,
진리는 합리주의 의존이고
인생은 진리의 수박 겉핥기이다.

인간은 체험만이 그것에 반역한다.
경력은 흥망성쇠의 골짜구니.
모든 자리는 세월의 액세서리.

내 친구는 거의 모든 것에,
통달했지만 모습이 바보고,
인생은 바보까지 관대하게 처분한다.

Prelude to life

A proverb is far more than any truth.
Truth depends on reasoning
and life's only a smattering of truth.

Experience of life rebels against that.
Life's history's composed of rise and fall.
All positions are the accesories of time.

My friend was well-versed
in almost everything, only he looked a fool,
and life deals generously even with fools.

선경仙境 1
    -풀

이 풀의 키는 약 1척이나 된다.
잎을 미묘히 늘어뜨린 모양은,
궁녀 같기도 하고 황후 같기도 하다.

빛깔은 푸른데 그냥 푸른 것이 아니고
농염미가 군데군데 끼인 채,
긴 잎을 늘어뜨리니 가관이다.

엷은 느낌이 날개 있으면 날 것 같고
유독히 그 자리에 자라난 것은,
흙 속에 뿌리박은 뿌리의 은덕이다.

Fairyland 1

—Grass

This grass is one foot high at least.
With its delicate dangling leaves it looks
like a lady-in-waiting, an empress, even.

It's green in hue, but no mere green,
darker and lighter here and there,
it's a fine sight with its dangling leaves.

I vaguely feel it would fly, given wings,
and that if it's growing in precisely that place
it's thanks to its roots plunging into the soil.

동창同窓

지금은 다 뭣들을 하고 있을까?
지금은 얼마나 출세를 했을까?
지금은 어디를 걷고 있을까?

점심을 먹고 있을까?
지금은 이사관이 됐을까?
지금은 가로수 밑을 걷고 있을까?

나는 지금 걷고 있지만,
굶주려서 배에서 무슨 소리가 나지마는
그들은 다 무엇들을 하고 있을까?

Classmates

What are they all doing now, I wonder?
How far have they got by now, I wonder?
Where are they walking now, I wonder?

Are they having lunch, I wonder?
Are they ranking officials, I wonder?
Are they walking under streetside trees, I wonder?

I'm walking now, but
my stomach's rumbling, I've not eaten;
what are they all doing now, I wonder?

길

가도 가도 아무도 없으니
이 길은 무인無人의 길이다.
그래서 나 혼자 걸어간다.
꽃도 피어 있구나.
친구인 양 이웃인 양 있구나.
참으로 아름다운 꽃의 생태여-
길은 막무가내로 자꾸만 간다.
쉬어 가고 싶으나
쉴 데도 별로 없구나.
하염없이 가니
차차 배가 고파온다.
그래서 음식을 찾지마는
가도 가도 무인지경이니
나는 어떻게 할 것인가?
한참 가다가 보니
마을이 아득하게 보여온다.
아슴하게 보여진다.
나는 더없는 기쁨으로
걸음을 빨리빨리 걷는다.
이 길을 가는 행복함이여.

Road

There's no one there, though I walk on and on,
this road is no one's road.
So I walk on alone.
Look, flowers in blossom!
Like friends, like neighbors!
Truly beautiful flowers' life-forms–
the road just keeps right on.
I'd like to snatch a moment's rest
but there's really no place much for that.
On and on I go until
bit by bit I get hungry.
I look for food but
though I walk on and on, it's no one's road,
what on earth shall I do?
After walking some more, at last
a village appears in the distance.
It comes into sight far away.
In unbridled joy I walk
quickly quickly along the road.
The bliss of going along this road!

약수터

내가 새벽마다 가는 약수터 가에는
천하선경이 아람드리 퍼진다.
요순堯舜이 놀까말까한 절대미경이라네.

하긴 그곳에 벌어지는 사물은 평범하지만,
그 조화미의 화목색和睦色은 순진하다네.

반드시 있을 곳에 자리잡고 있고,
운치와 조화와 빛깔이 혼연일치하니,
이 세계의 극치를 이루었다.

Beside a spring

Beside the spring I visit early every morning
spreads an expanse of earthly fairyland
a green land where Yao and Shun[*] might like to be.

All the plants you find there are ordinary enough
yet that lovely harmony's peaceful hue is so pure

everything is so exactly where it should be
grace, harmony and color are in such unity
that together they attain this world's perfection.

---

*Yao and Shun are the first Chinese kings mentioned in the "Book of Documents." Their reigns in the second millenium B.C. are traditionally seen as a golden age of harmony.

기쁨

친구가 멀리서 와,
재미있는 이야길 하면,
나는 킬킬 웃어 제낀다.

그때 나는 기쁜 것이다.
기쁨이란 뭐냐? 라고요?
허나 난 웃을 뿐.

기쁨이 크면 웃을 따름,
꼬치꼬치 캐묻지 말아라.
그저 웃음으로 마음이 찬다.

아주 좋은 일이 있을 때,
생색이 나고 활기가 나고
하늘마저 다정한 누님 같다.

Joy

If a friend arrives from far away
and tells entertaining tales
I giggle merrily.

Then I'm joyful.
So what is joy, you ask.
All I do is laugh.

The greater the joy, the greater the laughter.
Don't ask so many questions.
The heart is replete with simple laughter.

When something very good occurs
I feel gratified, envigorated
and the heavens seem like a loving sister to me.

희망

내일의 정상을 쳐다보며
목을 뽑고 손을 들어
오늘 햇살을 간다.

한 시간이 아깝고 귀중하다.
일거리는 쌓여 있고
그러나 보라 내일의 빛이

창이 앞으로 열렸다.
그 창 그 앞 그 하늘!
다만 전진이 있을 따름!

하늘 위 구름송이 같은 희망이여!
나는 동서남북 사방을 이끌고
발걸음도 가벼이 내일로 간다.

Hope

Gazing up at tomorrow's peaks
neck craned, hands raised,
I follow today's sunbeams.

Every hour is rare and precious.
Work may be piled up
but look, tomorrow's light.

The window's open on the future.
Before the window, what a sky!
Nothing but movement forwards!

Hope, like clouds high up in the sky!
North south east west every way
my steps move lightly towards tomorrow.

길

길은 끝이 없구나
강에 닿을 때는
다리가 있고 나룻배가 있다.
그리고 항구의 바닷가에 이르면
여객선이 있어서 바다 위를 가게 한다.

길은 막힌 데가 없구나
가로막는 벽도 없고
하늘만이 푸르고 벗이고
하늘만이 길을 인도한다.
그러니
길은 영원하다.

Road

Why, the road has no end.
When it touches a stream
there's a bridge or a ferry.
And when it reaches a seaside harbor
there are ships so we can cross the sea.

Why, there's nothing blocking the road.
There's no wall across it
and heaven alone is blue and a friend
heaven alone is guiding the road.
That means
the road is eternal.

흰구름

저 삼각형의 조그마한 구름이,
유유히 하늘을 떠다닌다.
무슨 볼 일이라도 있을까?
아주 천천히 흐르는 저것에는,
스쳐 지나는 바람이 있을 뿐이다.
바람은 구름의 연인이다.
그래서 바람이 부는 곳으로,
구름은 어김없이 간다.
희디흰 구름이여!
어느 계절이든지,
구름은 전연 상관 않는다.
오늘이 내일이 되듯이
구름은 유유하게 흐른다.

White cloud

That triangular little cloud
floats on at its leisure across the sky.
It may have some business to deal with.
That very slowly flowing thing
has only the breezes skimming past.
The wind is the cloud's true love.
So the cloud invariably goes
wherever the wind is blowing it.
Snow-white cloud!
The cloud is not in the least concerned
about what season it is.
The cloud flows on at its leisure
just as today becomes tomorrow.

꽃은 훈장

꽃은 훈장이다.
하느님이 인류에게 내리신 훈장이다.
산야에 피어 있는 꽃의 아름다움.

사람은 때로 꽃을 따서 가슴에 단다.
훈장이니까 할 수 없는 일이다.
얼마나 의젓한 일인가.

인류에게 이런 은총을 내린 하느님은
두고 두고 축복되어 마땅한 일이다.
전진을 거듭하는 인류의 슬기여.

A flower's a medal

A flower's a medal.
A medal awarded us by God.
The beauty of flowers in bloom on hills and plains.

Sometimes people pick flowers to wear on their breasts.
It's only natural, since they're medals.
It's a very admirable gesture.

It's natural to bless God for ever and ever
for bestowing such gracious awards on us.
Such is our wisdom that keeps advancing.

무덤

동양의 무덤은 자연주의 같고
서양의 무덤은 합리주의 같고
동양의 무덤은 지연합일 地然合一 이고
서양의 무덤은 편리위주이고

풀과 흙,
부드러운 선과 부피
아름드리 고요한 분위기,
이것이 우리 무덤의 모습이고-

빈틈없이 짜여진 공간 속에
되도록 조그마한 부피로 섰는 십자가
찾는 사람 별로 없는 곳
이것이 코쟁이의 무덤 모습이고-

우리 집 산소는
경남 창원군 진북면
대티마을 뒷산인데
일 년에 한 번씩 설날에 찾아간다.

Tombs

Oriental tombs are naturalistic
western tombs are rationalistic.
Oriental tombs are a union with earth
western tombs are convenience.

Grass and soil
gentle outline and volume
an armful of quiet atmosphere
that's our tombs...

Crammed together in a well-organized space
with a cross as small as possible
in a spot almost nobody visits
those are the white men's tombs...

Our family tombs
are on a hillside behind Daeti Village
in the Chinbuk district of Changwŏn county
in South Kyŏngsang province.
We visit them once a year on New Year's Day.

천상 시인
A Real Poet

날개

날개를 가지고 싶다.
어디론지 날 수 있는
날개를 가지고 싶다.
왜 하느님은 사람에게
날개를 안 다셨는지 모르겠다.
내 같이 가난한 놈은
여행이라고는 신혼여행뿐이었는데
나는 어디로든지 가고 싶다.
날개가 있으면 소원성취다.
하느님이여,
날개를 주소서 주소서……

Wings

I want wings.
I want wings
that will carry me wherever I want.
I can't understand why God
didn't give humans wings.
Being a pauper,
the only trip I've ever had was our honeymoon
but I want to go any and everywhere.
Once I have wings I'll be satisfied.
God
give me wings, please...

먼 산山

나는 의정부시에 사는데
먼 산이 바라보이고
뭔가 내게 속삭이는 것 같고
나를 자꾸 부르는 것 같다.

게으른뱅이인 나는
찾아가지는 안 했지만
언젠가 한번은
놀러 갈까 한다.

먼 산은 아주 옛날처럼 보이고
할아버지 같기도 하고
돌아가신 분들 같기도 하고
황성옛터 같다.

Distant mountain

I live in Uijŏngbu and
there's a mountain in sight in the distance
that seems to be whispering to me.
All the time it seems to be calling me.

Lazybones as I am,
I've not got that far yet
but I'm thinking of making a visit
one day some time soon.

The distant mountain looks like the good old days
like an old, old man
or maybe like those already dead
like the site of an ancient castle.

고향

내 고향은 경남 진동鎭東,
마산에서 사십 리 떨어진 곳
바닷가이며
산천이 수려하다.

국교 1년 때까지 살다가 떠난
고향도 고향이지만
원체 고향은 대체 어디인가?
태어나기 전의 고향 말이다.

사실은 사람마다 고향타령인데
나도 그렇고 다 그런데,
태어나기 전의 고향타령이 아닌가?
나이 들수록 고향타령이다.

무無로 돌아가자는 타령 아닌가?
경남 진동으로 가잔 말이 아니라
태어나기 전의 고향-무無로의
고향타령이다. 초로初老의 절감切感이다.

Home*

My home town is Chindong in South Kyŏngsang province
a place some twelve miles from Masan
beside the sea
lovely with hills and streams.

Home town is home, despite the fact
that I left there as soon as I started school.
I wonder where my real home is?
My home before I was born, I mean.

Almost all the time everyone's talking of home,
and I'm just like anyone else,
home before birth, I mean.
The older I get, the more I talk about home.

I really mean going back into the void, I suppose.
Not back to Chindong, that's sure.
To home before birth–home
back into the void. Middle–aged sensitivity.

*Ch'ŏn Sang Pyŏng was born in Japan, where his father had gone to work. But for Koreans, the "home town" is not necessarily the place where the individual was born, but the town or village in which recent generations of the family lived and were buried. The poet's family came back to their home village near Masan soon after his birth, then returned to Japan just when he was starting school. They finally returned home to Masan at the Liberation when the war ended in 1945.

Kyŏng-sang Province covers the south-eastern portion of the Korean Peninsula, Taegu and Pusan are the main cities, Masan is a port that lies to the west of Pusan along the southern coast.

구름

하늘에 둥둥 떠 있는 구름은
지상을 살피러 온 천사님들의
휴식처가 아닐까.

하느님을 도우는 천사님이시여
즐겁게 쉬고 가시고
잘되어 가더라고 말씀하소서.

눈에 안 보이기에
우리가 함부로 할지 모르오니
널리 용서하소서.

Clouds

Maybe the clouds that float in the sky
are armchairs for angels
come down to inspect the world?

Angel assistants of God
have a nice rest, then go
and tell him everything's fine.

You can't be seen
so we may misbehave;
I do hope you'll excuse us for that.

나의 가난함

나는 볼품없이 가난하지만
인간의 삶에는 부족하지 않다.
내 형제들 셋은 부산에서 잘 살지만
형제들 신세는 딱 질색이다.

각 문학사에서 날 돌봐주고
몇몇 문인들이 날 도와주고

그러니 나는 불편함을 모른다.
다만 하늘에 감사할 뿐이다.

이렇게 가난해도
나는 가장 행복을 맛본다.
돈과 행복은 상관없다.
부자는 바늘귀를 통과해야 한다.

My poverty

I may be shabbily poor,
I lack nothing a person needs in life.
My three brothers are living at ease in Pusan but
I wouldn't share their lot for anything.

My publishers look after me,
I get help from various writers

so I never experience the least discomfort.
I simply give thanks to Heaven, that's all.

I may be poor,
I enjoy the greatest happiness.
Money and happiness are unrelated.
The rich have to pass through a needle's eye.

아버지 제사祭祀

아버지 제삿날은 음력 구월 초사흗날
올해도 부산에 못 가니
또! 또!
아버님 영혼께서 화내시겠습니다.

가난이 천생天生인 것을
아버지 영혼이시여 살펴주소서
아버님도 생전에
"가난하게 살아야 복이 있다"고
하시지 않으셨습니까?

아버지는 젊을 때
천석千石꾼이었는데
일본놈에게 속아 다 날리고
도일渡日하여 돈을 버신 아버님.

아버지! 아버지!
지금까지 생존하였다면
팔십이 살짝 넘으셨을 아버지
오로지 천국에서 천복天福을 누리옵소서.

Offerings for father

We make offerings for father
on the third day of the ninth lunar month.
I can't get down to Pusan this year either
Again! Yet again!
Father's soul will be angry with me.

Dear father's soul, please remember
that poverty is heaven-sent.
Didn't you tell me
when you were alive,
"There's bliss in poverty?"

In his youth father's wealth
was a thousand sacks of rice a year
then fooled by the Japs he lost it all.
He went across to Japan to earn a living.

Father! Father!
If you were still alive now
you'd have just turned eighty; father,
I beg you, enjoy peace and joy in heaven.

찬물

나는 찬물 잘도 마십니다.
'물민족'이라며, 자꾸자꾸 마십니다.
그러면 생기生氣가 솟구치며
남들에게 뒤지지 않게 됩니다.

자연의 정기精氣를, 멀기는 하지만
흉내라도 내야 할 일이겠습니다.
만주의 송화강을 건너서
남쪽으로 올 때
우리 선조들이
<물> <물> 했듯이-

하늘 나는 새처럼, 하늘투성처럼,
나는 그저 찬물투성입니다.
생기가 있어야
인생을 놓치지 않는 법입니다.

나의 노래는 미약하지만
그 노래 끝에는
반드시 찬물 생기가 있어서
먼 데까지 가지 않을까 생각합니다.

Cold water

I'm fond of cold water.
We're "water people" so I keep on drinking.
Energy comes welling up
there I'm second to none.

Nature's energies are far from us
but still we must imitate all we can
like our ancestors
calling out "Water! Water!"
as they crossed Manchuria's Sungari River
in their progress southward.

Like birds that fly on, drenched in sky,
I'm all drenched in water.
Energy's essential
if we're not to let life slip through our fingers.

My song may be feeble,
at its end
I invariably find cold water energy
that can reach places far away.

광화문 근처의 행복

광화문에,
옛 이승만 독재와
과감하게 투쟁했던 신문사
그 신문사의 논설위원인
소설가 오상원은 나의 다정한 친구.

어쩌다 만나고픈 생각에
전화걸면
기어코 나의 단골인
'아리랑' 다방에 찾아온 그,
모월 모일, 또 그랬더니
와서는 내 찻값을 내고
그리고 천 원짜리 두 개를 주는데-
나는 그 때

Happiness near Kwanghwa-mun

At Kwanghwa-mun
there's the office of a paper that bravely fought
against the former dictator Syngman Rhee.*
That paper's leader writer,
the novelist Oh Sang-won, is a close friend of mine.

A man who, if I feel I want to see him
and ring him up,
unfailingly comes out to join me
in my regular coffee-shop Arirang.
One such day in such and such a month,
once again he came, paid for what I'd consumed
and offered me two thousand-won notes...
at which I said,

---

*Syngman Rhee was the first president of the Republic of Korea, from 1948 until 1960. His authoritarianism earned him increasing unpopularity until opposition to him culminated in the revolts of April 1960 which he tried to quell by violence. The April 19th Massacre, when the army fired on a crowd of unarmed students, brought about his downfall.

The Liberal Party was the party supporting the authoritarian rule of Syngman Rhee in the 1950s.

"오늘만은 나도 이렇게 있다"고
포켓에서 이천 원 끄집어 내어
명백히 보였는데도,
"귀찮아! 귀찮아!"하면서
자기 단골 맥주집으로 길을 가던 사나이!
그 단골집은
얼마 안 떨어진 곳인데
자유당 때 휴간休刊당하기도 했던
신문사의 부장 지낸 양반이
경영하는 집으로
셋이서
그리고 내 마누라까지 참석케 해서
자유와 행복의 봄을 -
꽃동산을 -
이룬 적이 있었습니다.

하느님!
저와 같은 버러지에게
어찌 그런 시간이 있게 했습니까?

"Just this once I'm afloat too,"
pulled out two thousand won from my pocket
and showed them to him plainly
but he just repeated, "It's alright, it's alright,"
heading for his regular beer house!
That bar
was not far away
it was run by a fellow who'd been section head
in a paper banned under the Liberal Party
and so the three of us,
my wife as well,
had a chance to celebrate
a springtime of freedom and happiness
a garden of flowers.

Dear God!
How could you let such a moment happen
to a poor wretch like me?

빛

태양의 빛 달의 빛 전등의 빛
빛은 참으로 근사하다.

빛이 없으면
다 캄캄할 것이 아닌가

세상은 빛으로 움직이고
사람 눈은 빛으로 있다

내일이여 내일이여
빛은 언제나 있으소서.

Light

Sunlight, moonlight, lamplight,
light's a really splendid thing.

Without light
everything would be dark, you know.

The world moves by light
human eyes exist by light.

Tomorrow, tomorrow,
let there always be light!

술

나는 술을 좋아한다.
그것도 막걸리로만
아주 적게 마신다.

술에 취하는 것은 죄다.
죄를 짓다니 안될 말이다.
취하면 동서사방을 모른다.

술은 예수 그리스도님도 만드셨다.
조금씩 마신다는 건
죄가 아니다.

인생은 고해苦海다.
그 괴로움을 달래 주는 것은
술뿐인 것이다.

Drink

I like a drink.
Only makkolli though,
and very little of that.

Getting drunk's a sin.
It's wrong to sin.
If I'm drunk I don't know where I am.

Even Jesus Christ made wine.
It's no sin
to drink just a little.

Out life's a vale of tears.
In order to reduce the pain
there's nothing like a drink.

유리창

창은 다 유리로 되지만
내 창에서는
나무의 푸른잎이다.

생기 활발한 나뭇잎
하늘을 배경으로
무심하게도 무성하게 자랐다.

때로는 새도 날으고
구름이 가고
햇빛 비치는 이 유리창이여-

Window pane

Windows are always made of glass
yet for my window I have
the green leaves of trees.

The vigorous lively leaves
with the sky as their background
grew up indifferent and thick.

Sometimes birds fly past
or a cloud goes by
Ah, this sunlit window pane...

바람에게도 길이 있다

강하게 때론 약하게
함부로 부는 바람인 줄 알아도
아니다! 그런 것이 아니다!

보이지 않는 길을
바람은 용케 찾아간다.
바람길은 사통팔달四通八達이다.

나는 비로소 나의 길을 가는데
바람은 바람길을 간다.
길은 언제나 어디에나 있다.

The wind has paths too

I think the wind blows at random
strongly and sometimes weakly
but it's not true! It's not at all like that!

The wind bravely follows
invisible paths.
Wind paths lie in all directions.

While I keep on along my path
the wind pursues its own wind-paths.
The path is always everywhere there.

구름

저건 하늘의 빈털터리 꽃
뭇사람의 눈길 이끌고
세월처럼 유유하다.

갈 데만 가는 영원한 나그네
이 나그네는 바람 함께
정처없이 목적없이 천천히

보면 볼수록 허허한 모습
통틀어 무게 없어 보이니
흰색 빛깔로 상공上空 수놓네.

Cloud

Look at the sky's own vagabond flower
attracting every gaze,
as leisurely as time.

Eternal wanderer, going where it likes
this wanderer moving with the wind
without a goal, without a purpose, slowly

seeming altogether weightless
blanker the longer you look at it
is embroidering the sky with tints of white.

노래

나는 아침 다섯 시가 되면
산으로 간다.
서울 북부인 이 고장은
지극한 변두리다.
산이 아니라
계곡이라고 해야겠다.
자연스레 노래를 부른다.

내같이 노래를 못 부르는 내가
목청껏 목을 뽑는다.
바위들도 그 묵직한 바위들도
춤을 추는 양하고
산등성이가 몸을 움직이는 양하고
새소리들도 내게 음악을 주고
나무들도 속삭이는 것 같다
나는 노래한다 나는 노래한다.

Singing

At five every morning
I go to the mountain.
It lies in northern Seoul
right on the city outskirts.
I don't mean a mountain at all
I ought really to say a valley.
There I sing freely.

Bad at singing as I am
I let rip.
And the rocks, those very serious rocks,
pretend to dance
the mountain ridges pretend to rock
while the birdsong gives me music
and the trees seem to whisper.
I'm singing, I'm singing.

요놈 요놈 요 이쁜 놈!

You lovely fellow, you!

행복

나는 세계에서
제일 행복한 사나이다.

아내가 찻집을 경영해서
생활의 걱정이 없고
대학을 다녔으니
배움의 부족도 없고
시인이니
명예욕도 충분하고
이쁜 아내니
여자 생각도 없고
아이가 없으니
뒤를 걱정할 필요도 없고
집도 있으니
얼마나 편안한가
막걸리를 좋아하는데
아내가 다 사주니
무슨 불평이 있겠는가
더구나
하나님을 굳게 믿으니
이 우주에서
가장 강력한 분이
나의 빽이시니
무슨 불행이 온단 말인가!

Happiness

I'm the happiest man
in the world.

Since my wife runs a café
I've no need to worry about making ends meet
and I went to university
so there's nothing lacking in my education
and because I'm a poet
my desire for fame is satisfied
I have a pretty wife too
so I don't think about women
and we have no children
no need to worry about the future
we have a house as well
I'm really very comfortable.
I'm fond of makkolli
my wife always buys it for me
so what have I got to complain of?
Besides
I firmly believe in God
and since the mightiest person
in the whole wide world
is looking after my interests
how can anyone say misfortune's coming?

들국화

84년 10월에 들어서
아내가 들국화를 꽃꽂이 했다.
참으로 방이 환해졌다.
하얀 들국화도 있고
보라색 들국화도 있고
분홍색 들국화도 있다.

가을은 결실의 계절이라고 하는데
우리 방은 향기도 은은하고
화려한 기색이 돈다
왜 이렇게도 좋은가
자연의 오묘함이 찾아들었으니
나는 일심一心으로 시 공부를 해야겠다.

Wild asters

One day early in October '84
my wife brought home a bunch of wild asters.
It made the room really bright.
There were white asters
and violet asters
and pink asters too.

Autumn's the season of mellow fruitfulness,
our room's lightly perfumed,
there's a marvellous feeling about.
Why is it so good?
Nature's profundity has come visiting,
I'll have to study poetry more.

아침

아침은 매우 기분 좋다
오늘은 시작되고
출발은 이제부터다

세수를 하고 나면
내 할 일을 시작하고
나는 책을 더듬는다

오늘은 복이 있을지어다
좋은 하늘에서
즐거운 소식이 있기를

Morning

Mornings I feel happiest.
Today has begun
the start's from now on.

Once I've finished washing my face
I begin my work
I grope for my books.

May there be blessings today.
May kind heaven send
some joyful news.

비

비가 내린다 비가 내린다
우수를 씹고 있는 나는
돌아가신 분들을 생각한다

비는 슬픔의 강물이다
내 젊은 날의 뉘우침이며
하느님의 보살피심을

친구들의 슬픈 이야기가
새삼스레 생각나누나
교회에 혼자 가서 기도할까나.

Rain

Rain falling, rain falling.
Ruminating melancholy
I recall the dead.

Rain is waters of sadness
repentance for my youth
God's providence.

Friends' sad plights
spring suddenly to mind.
Shall I go to church alone and pray?

먼 산山

먼 산은
나이 많은 영감님 같다
그 뒤는 하늘이고
슬기로운 말씀하신다

사람들은 다 제각기이고
통일은 없지만
하늘의 이치를 알게 되면
달라지리라고-

먼 산은
애오라지 역사의 거울
우리 인간은
그 침묵에서 배워야 하리……

Distant mountain

That distant mountain
is like an old man.
It has heaven behind it
speaking words of wisdom.

People all exist separately
there's no unity and yet
if once they learn the ways of heaven
it seems that makes a difference...

Distant mountain
history's only bigwig
we human beings
should learn from your silence...

촌놈

나는 의정부시 변두리에 살지만
서울과는 80미터 거리다
그러니 서울과 교통상으로는
별다름이 없지만
바로 근처에 논과 밭이 있으니
나는 촌놈인 것이다
서울에 살면
구백만 명 중의 한 사람이지만
나는 이제 그렇지가 않다.
촌놈은 참으로 행복하다
나는 노래 불러야 한다
이 대견한 행복을
어찌 노래 부르지 않으리요
하늘이여 하늘이여
나의 노래는 하늘의 것입니다.

Country bumpkin

I live on the outskirts of Uijŏngbu
but Seoul City's* only eighty yards away
and that's no big deal
as far as transport goes
but with rice and vegetable fields nearby
I'm a country bumpkin.
If you live in Seoul
you're just one among nine million
but that's not my case at all.
A country bumpkin's a happy man.
I must sing.
How could I not sing the praises
of such intense satisfaction?
Heaven! Heaven!
My song's heaven's own.

*The limits of Seoul City are marked by monumental markers placed along the main roads, so that travellers are always aware of the point where they leave the city limits.

꽃빛

손바닥 펴
꽃빛아래 놓으니
꽃빛 그늘 앉아 아롱집니다.

며칠 전 간
비원에서 본
그 꽃빛생각 절로 납니다.

그 밝음과 그늘이
열렬히 사랑하고 있습니다!
내 손바닥 위에서……

Flower hues

Look, my open hand
placed beneath these growing flowers
is mottled with flower-hued shade

inspiring unprompted memories, hues
of flowers seen in the Secret Garden[*]
when I was there a few days ago.

That brightness and shade
passionately making love!
Right on my palm...

*The Secret Garden is the name given in modern times to the gardens lying behind Chang-dŏk Palace in Seoul.

내가 좋아하는 여자

내가 좋아하는 여자의 으뜸은
물론이지만
아내이외일 수는 없습니다.

오십 둘이나 된 아내와
육십살 먹은 남편이니
거의 무능력자이지만

그래도 말입니다.
이 시 쓰는 시간은
89년 5월 4일
오후 다섯시 무렵이지만요-.

이, 삼일 전날 밤에는
뭉클 뭉클
어떻게 요동을 치는지

옆방의 아내를
고함 지르며 불렀으나,
한참 불러도

아내는 쿨쿨 잠자는 모양으로
장모님의
"시끄럽다-, 잠좀 자자"라는

The women I like

The first of all the women I like
can only be my wife
of course.

My wife's fifty-two
and I'm sixty now—
there's almost nothing we can do

but still!
The time as I write this poem
is five o'clock in the afternoon
of May the fourth 1989, but all the same...

Only two or three days ago, at night,
up and down, up and down,
there was suddenly such a squirming

that I called out in a loud voice
to my wife in the room next to mine;
I called and called

but she went on sleeping.
At last my mother-in-law called out,
"What a racket... let's get some sleep"

말씀 때문에
금시 또 미꾸라지가 되는 걸
필자는 어쩌지 못했어요-.

and thanks to those words
I went back to being a loach again
with no hope of even beginning.

달

달을 쳐다보며 은은한 마음,
밤 열 시경인데 뜰에 나와
만사를 잊고 달빛에 젖다.

우주의 신비가 보일 듯 말 듯
저 달에 인류의 족적이 있고
우리와 그만큼 가까워진 곳.

어릴 때는 멀고 먼 곳
요새는 만월이며 더 아름다운 것
구름이 스치듯 걸려 있네.

Moon

Gazing up at the moon with a heart serene
I'm out in the fields though it's ten at night
forgetting life's cares and soaking in moonlight.

Whether or not the mysteries of space can be seen
there's a human footprint up on that moon
that place that's become so close to us

that place so far away far when I was a child
now it's full moon and more beautiful still
the clouds cling close as if brushing against it.

마음 마을

내 마음의 마을을
구천동이라 부른다.
내가 천씨요 구천九千만큼
복잡다단한 동네다.

비록 동네지만
경상남도보다 더 넓고
서울특별시도 될 만하고
또 아주 조그만 동네밖에 안 될 때도 있다.

뉴욕의 마천루摩天樓 같은
고층건물이 있는가 하면
초가지붕도 있고
태고시대太古時代의 동굴도 있다.

이 마을 하늘에는
사시장철 새가 날아다니고
그렇지 않을 때는
흰구름이 왕창 덮인다.

이 마을 법률은
양심이 있을 뿐이고
재판소 따위로는
양심법 재판소밖에는 없다.

Heart's village

My heart's village
is called Nine Thousand Village.
I'm Mr. Thousand, but it's a neighborhood
crowded and busy enough for nine thousand.

True, it's only one neighborhood
but it's vaster than South Kyŏngsang Province
equal to the City of Seoul yet at the same time
nothing more than one very small neighborhood.

Yes, it has high buildings
like the skyscrapers of New York,
but it has thatched cottages
and caves from prehistoric times, too.

In this village's sky
birds of every season fly,
and when that is not the case
white clouds cover it completely.

This village's law
is conscience alone
for its court-house
there's nothing but the court of conscience.

여러 가지로 지적하려면
만자萬字도 모자란다
복잡하고 복잡한 이 마음 마을이여

If you want to point out this and that
ten thousand words will not suffice.
This heart's complex crowded village.

계곡 흐름

나는 수락산 아래서 사는데,
여름이 되면
새벽 5시에 깨어서
산 계곡으로 올라가
날마다 목욕을 한다.
아침마다 만나는 얼굴들의
제법 다정한 이야기들.

큰 바위 중간 바위 작은 바위.
그런 바위들이 즐비하고
나무도 우거지고
졸졸졸 졸졸졸
윗바위에서 떨어지는 물소리.

더러는 무르팍까지
잠기는 물길도 있어서……
(내가 가는 곳은 그런 곳)
목욕하고 있다 보면
계곡 흐름의 그윽한 정취여……

Flowing stream

I live below Mount Surak.
In summer
I wake at five
climb up to a mountain stream
and wash there every day.
The really kind things said by
the faces I meet each morning.

Big rocks, middling rocks, small rocks
such rocks are plentiful
and the trees grow thick
gurgle gurgle gurgle
the sound of water dropping from the rocks.

There's sometimes water
splashing as high as my knees...
(that's the kind of place I go)
as I'm washing,
the secluded mood of the flowing stream...

오월의 신록

오월은 신록의 달이다.
파란 빛이
온 세상을 덮는 오월은
문자 그대로 신록의 달이다.

파란 빛은 눈에 참 좋다.
눈에 좋을 뿐만 아니라
희망을 속삭여 준다.

오월 달은 그래서
너무 짧은 것 같다.
푸른 오월이여
세계의 오월이여

Maytime greenery[*]

May's the month for greenery.
Green light
covering the world, Maytime's
literally the month for greenery.

Green light's very good for the eyes.
And not just for the eyes;
it whispers of hope.

So the month of May
seems much too brief.
Green Maytime!
All the world's Maytime!

*This was the last poem the poet wrote. It was found in the pocket of his coat after his death.

나의 詩作의 뜻

시작詩作의 의미를 대체大體로 밝히겠다. 한 편 한 편의 시작 노트를 지면 관계로 쓸 수는 없지만 전체적인 시작 과정은 쓸 수 있다.

나는 시를 문학의 왕이라고 생각한다. 문학이라고 하면 장르도 많다. 소설도 있고 수필도 있고 아동문학도 있고 희곡도 있고 가지가지다. 그런데 시는 그 중에서도 으뜸이라는 것이다.

시는 가장 진실하다는 것이다. 거짓말하는 시는 시가 아니다. 시는 가장 진실의 진실이다. 우리는 진실을 떠나서는 살 수 없다.

기쁨도 진실의 한 의미이다. 나는 웃음을 좋아한다. 김주연이라는 평론가는 시평詩評에서 나의 시를 두고 웃음이 안 나올 수 없다고 평했는데, 웃음이 나오는 시를 나는 일부러 쓴 적이 없지만 그래도 유머를 감각할 수 있는 모양이다.

여러 독자들이여. 우리는 진실을 위하여 살고 있습니다. 인생의 진실은 여기저기에 깔려 있습니다. 이것을 표현하는 것이 시입니다. 시를 읽고 짜증을 낸다면 그 시는 가짜입니다!

나는 이런 시는 쓰지 않았다. 되도록 인생의 참뜻을 알리려고 했다.

나는 시를 단시간에 쓰는 편이다. 그러나 쓸 때만이 단시간이지 그 시를 구상하는 데는 많은 시일이 걸린다. 한번 착상을 하면 이렇게 쓸까 저렇게 쓸까 하고 많은 시일이 걸린다.

시작노트는 그 시의 생명이다. 이렇게 되어서 이 시가 생겼소, 하고 말하는 것은 쉬운 일이 아니다.

그것은 본질을 말하는 것이기 때문이다.

나는 시를 인생의 본질이라고 말했다. 우리는 한 가지 일에 충실해야 한다. 그래서 우수한 작품이 만들어질 수가 있는 것이다.

나는 아이가 없어서 그런지 더욱 고독하다. 이 고독을 극복하자면 자연히 든든해야 한다. 그러자면 자연히 굳세어야 한다.

그래서 언제나 센 마음으로 이 인생을 솔직하게 대하고, 굳세어야 하는 것이다.

굳세자니 책을 많이 읽어야 하는 것이다. 책을 많이 읽는 것뿐만 아니라 생각도 많이 하기 마련이다. 그래서 여러 가지 생각을 해야 한다.

그래서 시와 가깝게 지내고 있다. 가깝게 지내자니 자연히 시와 관계가 많아진다. 그래서 시인이 된지도 모른다.

시인인 내가 조심해야 할 것은, 아무것도 아닌 가치없는 일에 사로잡힐까 그것이 걱정이다. 되도록 인생에 큰 무게를 주는 사실에 치중하여 그것을 시에 반영해야 하는 것이다.

나는 고독해야 하기 때문에 언제나 음산할 수밖에 없을 것이라고 생각하기 쉽지만 그렇지 않다. 하느님이 계시기 때문이다. 나는 하느님을 믿는다.

하느님은 나의 절대絶對적 존재이다. 나는 고독할 때면 언제나 하느님을 생각하고 고독해지지 않으려고 한다.

그러니 어떻게 생각하면 언제나 고독하지 않다고 생각할 수도 있다.

나의 시에서 무고독을 생각하는 것은 일면의 진실이 있다. 우리는 언제나 있는 하느님을 믿음으로써 고독하지 않다. 하느님은 언제나 나를 위로해 주신다.

나는 언제나 시를 나의 생활 주변에서 찾는 것이 버릇이다. 생활 주변은 항상 시에 가득차 있는 것이다. 여러분 똑똑한 눈으로 생활 주변을 보면 시가 구르고 있는 것이다.

생활은 넓다. 가만히 혼자 있어도 시는 있는 것이다. 눈을 뜨고 있는 한 시는 언제나 구르고 있는 것이다. 이것을 잡기만 하면 시는 태어난다.

나는 생활을 사랑한다. 하잘것없는 일상에서도 무엇을 느끼게 하는 것은 많은 것이다. 이런 일상의 습성에서 나는 용케도 시를 잡는 것이다.

일상생활의 하잘것없는 물건이나 사건에서조차 시를 찾는 나는 풍부한 시적 소재를 잡는 것이다. 모든 것에서 나는 많은 테마를 얻는 것이다.

나의 가족이라고는 아내 단 한 사람뿐이고 쓸쓸한 편이지만, 모든 것을 사랑하라는 하느님의 말씀에 순종하는 나는 외롭지 않다.

너무 외로우면 시를 못쓰는 것이다. 이거나 저거나 다 나와 무관하지 않다고 생각하는 나는 행복한 것이다. 돈도 못 벌고 아내밖에 없는 내가 비교적 낙관적인 것은 이 때문이다.

생활은 복잡하지만 그래도 정신을 가다듬고 정리하면 아주 단순한 것이다. 생활을 단순하다고 생각하는 사람은 드물겠지만 나는 그 중의 한 사람이다.

시의 소재는 의미있는 일에만 있는 것이 아니다. 아무렇지도 않은 일에서 나는 깊은 의미를 찾는 버릇이 있다.

하여튼 나는 나의 생활 주변에서 일어나는 모든 일에서 멋을 찾고 그리고 그것을 형상화한다. 그래서 하찮은 일이 나의 시가 되는 것이다.

아무쪼록 나는 맑은 눈으로 생활을 직시하고 있는 것이다. 그래서 하찮은 것들에서 나는 시를 찾고 있다. 그래서 생활은 나의 시인 것이다.

나는 음악을 사랑하고 있다. 그것도 고전음악이다. 그래서 나는 시를 쓸 때면 언제나 KBS의 FM 방송을 틀고 귀를 기울인다. 이 방송은 하루종일 고전음악을 방송하는 것이다.

아름다운 음악은 시상詩想을 깨우칠 뿐만 아니라 합당한 어귀를 제공하는 것이다. 음악 없는 나의 시는 생각할 수조차 없다. 아름다움은 시의 생명인 것이다.

세계는 복잡하다. 전쟁도 있고 평화도 있는 이 세계의 소용돌이야말로 우리 생활 감정을 복잡하게 하지만 정신만 똑바로 세우면 간단한 것이 된다. 그 영향이 생활에 미쳐지게 되는 것이다.

이런 세계적인 일에서 생활은 영향을 아니받을 수 없다. 이 영향 관계도 생활 속에 미쳐지고 있는 것이다. 그러나 생활을 직시하면 이런 것들이 모두 판가름나는 것이다. 하여튼 생활을 직시할 일이다. 인생은 생활인 것이다. 인생의 진실이란 생활 안에 있고 그리고 그 대표적인 것이다.

내가 쓴 옛날의 시에 「푸른 것만이 아니다」란 시가 있다. 푸른 빛깔 속에는 푸른 빛깔만이 아닌 색깔도 있다는 시다. 한 가지 사물 속에는 한 가지만이 아닌 것들이 있는 것이다.

어쨌든 나는 나의 믿음과 생활이 나의 시의 근본이라고 말했다. 이것은 곧 나의 시적 태도이며 근본인 것이다.

우리는 시를 읽으면서, 어렵다고 생각해서는 안 된다. 쉽게 생각해야 한다. 어렵다고 생각되는 시는 시가 아니다.

수필적으로 읽을 수 있는 시가 좋은 시라고 나는 생각한다. 사소로운 일에서 인생의 근본을 생각게 하는 것이 시다.

믿음과 생활은 시의 근본이라는 것이 나의 생각이다. 어려운 말이 개입될 여지가 나에게는 없는 것이다.

믿음은 절대자에 대한 신앙이다. 이 세계의 본질을 모르고 우리가 어떻게 살 것인가. 절대자가 있는데, 어떻게 우리가 모른 체 살 수 있겠는가?

믿음은 나의 인생의 최고 원리이다. 이 원리원칙을 빼고 어떻게 시를 쓸 수 있단 말인가. 나로 말하면 원리 없이는 너무나 무력한 존재인 것이다.

그래서 교회에도 나가고 시를 쓰는 것이다. 이 시집에서는 신앙시가 없다시피하다.

이 시집에는 요새 쓴 시와 예전에 쓴 시가 섞여 있지만 독자들은 그런 줄 알고 읽어주었으면 좋겠다.

나는 이번 이 시집이 세 권째 시집이다. 나의 55세에 시집이 세 권뿐이라니 좀 적은 편이지만, 그래도 나는 후회하지 않는다.

가난하고 불쌍한 시인이지만 나는 후회없이 열심히 살고 있다. 사랑이야말로 인생의 행복인 것이다. 나는 가난하고 슬퍼도 행복한 것이다.

그 행복의 결과가 이 시집으로 태어난 것이다.

행복이란 딴 것이 아니다. 언제나 가슴 뿌듯하게 사는 것이 행복인 것이다. 사소한 일에서도 의미를 찾을 수 있고 그리고 기쁨을 느낀다면 그건 행복이다.

내가 그런 것이다. 여러분이 이 시집을 읽고 조금이라도 마음을 홀가분하게 해주신다면 필자에겐 더한 기쁨이 없겠다.

아무쪼록 시간나는 대로 읽으셔서 기쁨을 억지로라도 찾아주십시오, 하는 게 필자의 바램이자 소망이다.

천상병(千祥炳)

Notes on Writing Poetry

Let me expose briefly how I write poetry. There is no room for detailed notes on the composition of each individual poem, but I can explain how I see poetry-writing in general terms.

I consider poetry to be the king of literature. In literature there are many different genres: you have novels, essays, childrens' stories, drama. But poetry is topmost among them.

By that I mean that poetry is the truest of all. A lying poem is no poem. A poem is the truest of all truths. We cannot live if once we abandon truth.

Joy is one expression of truth. I love to laugh. The critic Kim Ju-Yon once commented that he could not help laughing when he read my work; I have never deliberately written poems to make people laugh but there does seem to be a sense of humour about them.

You and I are all living for the sake of truth. The truth about human existence lies spread far and wide. What gives it expression is poetry. If you get angry after reading a poem, it must have been a fake!

I never write poems like that. More and more with the passage of time I have tried to express the true meaning of human existence.

I tend to write poems quickly. But it is only the writing down of the poem that is soon done; it takes a long time for me to compose a poem. Once I have hit on an idea, I spend hours reflecting whether I should express it in this way or that.

Notes on the composition of a poem touch its very being. It is very difficult to say, such a poem came in being for this particular reason. Because then you are expressing its very essence.

As I said, I see poetry as the essence of human existence. We have to be faithful to one particular task. Only then is it possible for worthwhile works to be produced.

Perhaps because I have no children, I am rather lonesome. In order to overcome that loneliness I naturally have to become stronger. Which naturally means I have to become more firmly resolved.

I am obliged to face existence honestly, with a bold heart, since in that way I grow more resolved.

Wishing to become more resolved means that I have to read a lot of books. Not only do I have to read many books, I have to do a lot of thinking too.

As a result, I have to live in close contact with poetry. Wishing to live in close contact with it, naturally my links with poetry multiply. Maybe that is why I became a poet.

What I have to be careful of as a poet is my fear of being snared by worthless things of no value. Attaching importance to the realities that give increasing weight to human existence as time goes by, I have to reflect that in my poems.

It is easy to imagine that since I am obliged to lead a lonely existence, I must be gloomy all the time but such is not the case.

That is because God is there. I believe in God.

God is the absolute being for me. Whenever I feel lonely, I think of God and try not to feel lonely.

That is as much as to say that I never feel lonely at all.

The thought that I am never lonely is one aspect of the truth in my poetry. Thanks to belief in the constant presence of God, I am never lonely. God is always there comforting me.

I have got into the habit of constantly looking out for poetry in my everyday surroundings. Our surroundings are full of poetry.

If you look at your own life's surroundings properly, you're sure to find a poem rolling around.

Life covers a wide area. Even when you are somewhere quietly on your own, there is poetry about. You only need open your eyes, there is a poem rolling around. You just have to seize it for a poem to be born.

I love being alive. Even in the trivial incidents of daily life there are so many moments when you feel something. I have grown quite good at seizing poems in the thick of daily living.

I look for poetry in the trivial things and incidents of everyday life, and as a result I find myself with a plentiful supply of material for poems. I find so many things to write about in everything around me.

As far as family goes, there is no one but my wife so it's

a bit deary but I'm never alone since I try to follow God's command to love everyone.

If you are too much alone you cannot write poetry. I'm blessed because I consider that there is nothing that does not concern me. That explains why I am relatively optimistic, although I cannot earn any money and have nobody in life except my wife.

Life may be complicated, if only you keep your wits calm and steady, it is really very simple. There may not be many people who think life is simple, but I am one of them.

Material for poems is not only found in deeply meaningful events. I have got into the habit of finding deep meaning in quite insignificant happenings.

I savor intensely everything that happens around me and try to give it shape. In that way trivial events turn into poems.

I face life with open eyes and that is why I find poetry in insignificant things. So life is my poetry.

I love music. Classical music. So whenever I am writing a poem I always listen to the radio. There is a channel that broadcasts classical music all day long.

Beautiful music not only stimulates poetic ideas, it furnishes an appropriate approach. I cannot even imagine writing without music. Beauty is the very life of a poem.

The world is a complex place. This world's mixture of war and peace complicates our emotions about life but so long as we keep our minds straight, everything is simple. The effect of all that has an influence on the world.

Our life is bound to be affected by the things that happen in the world. Those influences are reflected in our lives. If we face life squarely, such things are decisive. Or at least, facing life squarely is. Life needs to be lived. The truth about existence lies in our lives and characterises them.

There is a poem I wrote a long time ago called "Not just blue". It is about how there are other colors, not only the color blue, in the color blue. There are other things, not only one thing, in each object.

As I have said, my life and my faith are the basis for my poetry. That is my approach to poetry and its very essence.

It is no good if we think how difficult a poem is, as we read it. The thought must be simple. A poem we have difficulty with is no poem.

I consider that a poem we can read like an essay is a good poem. A poem is something that makes us think about the essence of existence on the basis of some trifling incident.

I think that faith and life are the essence of poetry. For me there can be no excuse for the use of difficult words.

Faith is belief in the Absolute Being. How can we live if we do not know the essence of the world? Since the Absolute exists, how can we live ignoring it?

Faith is the first principle of my existence. This fundamental principle once removed, I do not see how it is possible to write poetry. For myself, without principles I am helpless.

So I go to church and write poems. There are almost no

religious poems in this volume, though.

You will find here poems written recently and others written earlier, but readers need not worry about that.

This is my third book. At fifty-five, only to have published three books is not very much but I regret nothing.

I may be a poor wretched poet but I live as well as I can without any regrets. Love is the greatest happiness in life. I may be poor and sad, I am happy too.

This book is the outcome of that happiness.

Happiness is nothing other than that. Happiness means always living with a full heart. Happiness is when you are able to find meaning in trifles and feel happy.

That is how I am. If you are able to lighten your hearts even a little by reading these poems, nothing could give me greater joy.

Ch'ŏn Sang Pyŏng

『한국문학 영역총서』를 펴내며

　한국문학을 본격적으로 번역하여 해외에 소개하는 일이 필요함을 우리는 오래 전부터 절실히 느껴 왔다. 그러나 좋은 번역을 만나기는 좋은 창작품을 만나는 것 못지 않게 어렵다. 운이 좋아서 좋은 번역이 있을 경우에는 또한 출판의 기회를 얻기가 쉽지 않다. 서구의 유수한 출판사들은 시장성을 앞세워 지명도가 높지 않은 한국의 문학작품을 출판하기를 꺼린다. 한국문학의 지명도가 높아지려면 먼저 훌륭하게 번역된 작품들이 세계적인 명성이 있는 출판사에서 출판이 되어 널리 보급이 되어야 하는데, 설혹 훌륭한 번역이 있다 하더라도 이 작품들이 해외에서 출판될 기회가 극히 제한되어 있어서, 지명도를 높일 길이 막막해지는 악순환을 거듭하는 것이 현실이다. 이런 현실을 타개하는 길은 좋은 작품을 제대로 번역하여 우리 손으로 책답게 출판하여 세계의 독자들에게 내놓는 데서 찾을 수밖에 없다. 이런 일을 하기 위해 도서출판 답게에서 '한국문학 영역총서'를 세상에 내놓는다.

　'답게' 영역총서는 한영 대역판으로 출판되며, 이 총서는 광범위한 독자층을 위하여 만들어진 것이다. 무엇보다도 이 총서를 통해 해외의 많은 문학 독자들이 한국문학을 알게 되기를 희망한다. 이 총서는 또한 국내에서 한국학을 공부하거나 영어로 번역된 한국 작품을 필요로 하는 영어 사용권의 모든 사람들과 한국문학의 전문적인 번역자들을 위한 것이기도 하다. 전문 번역인들은 동료 번역자들의 작업을 자신들의 것과 비교함으로써 보다 나은 새로운 번역 방법을 모색할 수 있을 것이다. 고급한 영어를 배우기를 원하는 한국의 독자들도 대역판으로 출간되는 이 총서를 읽음으로써, 언어가 어떻게 문학적으로 신비롭게 또 절묘하게 쓰이는지를 깨닫는 등 많은 것을 얻을 수 있을 것이다.

아무리 말쑥하게 잘 만들어진 책이라도 그 내용이 신통치 않으면 결코 책다운 책일 수 없다는 자명한 이유에서, '답게' 영역총서는 좋은 작품을 골라 최선의 질로 번역한 책만을 출판할 것이다. 또한 새로운 번역자의 발굴과 격려가 이 총서 발간의 목적 가운데 하나이다. '답게' 출판사가 발행하는 이 총서가 한국문학 번역의 중요성을 다시 한 번 일깨우고, 문학 작품의 번역이라는 불가능한 꿈을 가능하게 하려는 번역자들의 노력에 보탬이 되기를 바란다. 이런 시도가 여러 가지로 유용하고 또 도전적인 것이 될 때, 더 나아가서는 잘 번역된 한국 작품의 전세계적인 출판 작업이 이루어지는 단초를 마련할 수 있을 때, 이 선구적인 계획은 진정으로 성공적인 것이 될 것이다.

김영무 (서울대 영문과 교수)

Series Editor's Afterword

Extensive translation of Korean literature for the foreign readers has for many years been felt a pressing need. But to fall upon a good translation is much harder than to discern a good original work. If we are fortunate enough to secure a good translation, it is often very difficult to get it published abroad.

The major publishers of the western world are not yet prepared to run the risk of publishing works of relatively unknown Korean literature. Yet if Korean literature is to achieve worldwide fame, it first of all needs to be well translated, and then put into circulation throughout the world by those very publishers which are so reluctant to publish even good translations of Korean literature. It is a vicious circle : no publication without fame but no fame without publication. To save the situation, we should perhaps try to make available to readers abroad choice translations we ourselves have published in editions of high quality. The DapGae English Translations of Korean Literature series has been launched with this aim.

Each volume of the DapGae series will be a bilingual edition. We expect a wide-ranging audience for the series. It is our primary hope that it will help introduce many foreign readers to the world of Korean literature. The series is especially intended to serve English-speaking students enrolled in Korean studies programs and all who need translations of Korean literature, as well as those who may wish to compare their own translations with the translations of fellow translators in order to find new and better ways of translating. Korean readers studying advanced English can also benefit from reading these bilingual editions : the experi -ence may help them to recognize the mystery of true mastery of the literary use of language.

However well designed a book may be, it cannot properly serve its purpose if the contents are mediocre. For that reason, the DapGae series will strive to introduce to the readers of the world the best translations of the finest works of Korean literature. One of the objectives of the series is to find and encourage new talents in English translation. We hope that the DapGae English Translations of Korean Literature series will serve in some small way to refocus at- tention upon the importance of translating Korean literature into good English and to make possible the impossible dream of literary translation. This pioneering project will be a true success not only if it proves useful and challenging but also if it paves the way for the publication of fine translations of Korean literature on a worldwide scale.

Kim Young-Moo
Department of English
Seoul National University

역자소개 The translators

●안토니 수사
1942 영국의 콘월 지방 트루로에서 출생.
옥스포드 대학 퀸즈 칼리지에서 중세, 현대문학을 공부.
1969 프랑스 초교파 수도원 테제 공동체에 입회하여 수사가 됨.
1980 한국에 온 이래 다른 테제 수사들과 함께 서울에서 거주.
1991 대한민국 문학상 번역상 수상. 코리아 타임즈 시부문 번역상 수상.
1996 한국 펜클럽 번역상 수상.
현재 서강대학교 교수로 영문학 강의. 구상, 김광규, 고은, 천상병, 서정주 등의 시집을 영어로 번역 출간, 이문열의 소설『시인』을 영역하여 대산문학상 번역상 수상. 화엄경에 나오는 선재동자의 이름을 따서 안선재安善財라는 한국명도 가지고 있다.

●김영무
1944 경기도 파주 출생. 서울대학교 문리과대학에서 영문학 공부, 미국 뉴욕 주립 대학에서 영문학 박사학위 수여.
1991 평론집『삶의 언어와 시의 언어』로 대한민국 문학상 평론상 수상.
1993 첫 시집『색동 단풍숲을 노래하라』를 상재.
1998 산문집『제비꽃에 너를 보며』
시집『산은 새소리마저 쌓아두지 않는구나』
현재 서울대 영문과 교수.

Brother Anthony was born in Truro (UK) in 1942 and studied at Queen's College, Oxford University. He joined the Community of Taizé, France in 1969. He has been living in Korea since 1980. He is a professor in the English Department at Sogang University in Seoul. He is the translator of *Wastelands of Fire: Selected Poems by Ku Sang* and *A Korean Century: River and Fields, Poems by Ku Sang* (Forest Books, 1990), *Faint Shadows of Love: Selected Poems by Kim Kwang-kyu* (Forest Books, 1991), *The Sound of My Waves: Selected Poems by Ko Un* (Cornell East Asia Series, 1993), *Midang, So Chong-ju: The Early Lyrics* (Forest Books, 1998) and *Back to Heaven: Selected Poems by Ch'ŏn Sang-Pyŏng* (Cornell East Asia Series, 1995). His translations of poems by Kim Kwang-kyu were awarded the Grand Prix for Translation in the 1991 Korean National Literary Awards. He was awarded the 1991 Korea Times Translation Prize for Poetry and the 1996 Korea PEN translation prize. He was also the co-translator of Yi Mun-yol's novel *The Poet* (The Harvill Press, 1995), which was awarded the 1995 Daesan Translation Award.

Kim Young-Moo was born in Seoul 1944 and studied English literature at Seoul National University. He received his Ph.D in English from the State University of New York at Stony Brook. He is professor of English literature at Seoul National University. He is the author of many critical essays on modern Korean literature; his first collection of poems *(The Autumn Forest)* was published in 1993. He was awarded the Grand Prix for Literary Criticism in the 1990 Korean National Literary Awards with his collection of critical essays, *The Language of Poetry and the Language of Life*. He is the co-translator of *The Sound of My Waves: Selected Poems by Ko Un* (Cornell East Asia Series, 1993) and *Back to Heaven: Selected Poems by Ch'ŏn Sang-Pyŏng* (Cornell East Asia Series, 1995)

귀천 *Back to Heaven*

지은이 | 천 상 병
옮긴이 | 안토니 · 김영무
펴낸이 | 一庚 張 少 任
펴낸곳 | 답게

초판 발행 | 1996년 9월 5일
재판 26쇄 | 2025년 2월 15일

등 록 | 1990년 2월 28일, 제 21-140호
주 소 | 04975 서울시 광진구 천호대로 698 진달래빌딩 502호
전 화 | (편집) 02)469-0464, 462-0464
         (영업) 02)463-0464, 498-0464
팩 스 | 02)498-0463
홈페이지 | www.dapgae.co.kr
e-mail | dapgae@gmail.com, dapgae@korea.com

ISBN 978-89-7574-144-3 (02810)
원작 ⓒ 1996, 천상병
번역 ⓒ 1996, 안토니 · 김영무

나답게 · 우리답게 · 책답게

* 책값은 뒤 표지에 있습니다.
* 잘못 만들어진 책은 구입하신 서점에서 교환해 드립니다.
* 이 책은 현재 미국 코넬 대학에서 한국학 교재로 사용하고 있습니다.